CELIA HILL'S HEADIN' WEST

BOOKS BY BILL WRIGHT

Across the Border and Back: Music in the Big Bend,
by Marcia Hatfield Daudistel with photographs by Bill Wright

A Bridge from Darkness to Light: Thirteen Young Photographers Explore Their Afghanistan

The Whole Damn Cheese: Maggie Smith, Border Legend

Authentic Texas: People of the Big Bend,
with Marcia Hatfield Daudistel

Fort Phantom Hill: The Mysterious Ruins on the Clear Fork of the Brazos River

Oman: Land of Diversity

The Texas Outback: Ranching on the Last Frontier,
with June Redford Van Cleef

People's Lives: A Photographic Celebration of the Human Spirit

Portraits from the Desert: Bill Wright's Big Bend

The Texas Kickapoo: Keepers of Tradition, with E. John Gesick Jr.

Stray Tales of the Big Bend, by Elton Miles with
photographs by Bill Wright

The Tiguas: Pueblo Indians of Texas

CELIA HILL'S HEADIN' WEST
TO A REMOTE CANYON PARADISE

CELIA HILL
with
Bill Wright *and*
Marianne Wood

FORT WORTH, TEXAS

Copyright © 2023 by Bill Wright and Marianne Wood

Library of Congress Cataloging-in-Publication Data

Names: Hill, Celia, 1928-2008, author. | Wright, Bill, 1933- author. | Wood, Marianne (Photographic assistant), author.
Title: Celia Hill's headin' west : to a remote canyon paradise / Celia Hill with Bill Wright and Marianne Wood.
Description: Fort Worth, Texas : TCU Press, [2023] | Includes bibliographical references. | Summary: "This collection of stories sets out a first-person account of a family who moved from Memphis, Tennessee, in the late 1800s to Hobart, Oklahoma, and then to Texas, back to Oklahoma and back again to Texas. The Oklahoma stint afforded a memory of Geronimo, so the indecision of the family bore this fruit, if no other. Through Celia Hill's lens we learn about life in the western part of Texas as she grew to become a competent cowgirl and later a schoolteacher. Except for an epilogue Celia wrote about a homecoming for the people who lived in Terlingua prior to 1946, we have nothing from her own hand about her life after 1945. But an interview by Bob Phillips of Texas Country Reporter in 2006 gives us more of her story and interviews with her son, Rusty Hill, fill in more gaps"— Provided by publisher.
Identifiers: LCCN 2022047228 (print) | LCCN 2022047229 (ebook) | ISBN 9780875658469 (paperback) | ISBN 9780875658476 (ebook)
Subjects: LCSH: Hill, Celia, 1928-2008—Travel—Texas, West—Diaries. | Hill family. | Texas, West—Description and travel. | Texas, West—Social life and customs—20th century. | Terlingua (Tex.)—Biography. | Pinto Canyon (Tex.)—Biography. | Big Bend Region (Tex.)—Biography. | LCGFT: Diaries. | Autobiographies.
Classification: LCC F391.4.H56 A3 2023 (print) | LCC F391.4.H56 (ebook) | DDC 976.4/06092 [B]—dc23/eng/20221007
LC record available at https://lccn.loc.gov/2022047228
LC ebook record available at https://lccn.loc.gov/2022047229

TCU Box 298300
Fort Worth, Texas 76129

Design by Preston Thomas

Cover photo: Special Smith Family photo. Courtesy of the family of Celia Hill.

CONTENTS

PREFACE *vii*
INTRODUCTION *by Bill Wright and Marianne Wood* 1
INTRODUCTION *by Celia Hill* 9
PROLOGUE 11

CHAPTER ONE
Life in Terlingua 17

CHAPTER TWO
Rare Commodities 21

CHAPTER THREE
Seven in One 27

CHAPTER FOUR
Johnson's Ranch 29

CHAPTER FIVE
Whistle While You Work 31

CHAPTER SIX
The Spring 35

CHAPTER SEVEN
Politics 37

CHAPTER EIGHT
Pink Glass—Russo 39

CHAPTER NINE
The Feed Bin and Border Patrol 41

CHAPTER TEN
Predator Control 43

CHAPTER ELEVEN
When the Dogs Bark 45

CHAPTER TWELVE
Wash Day Blues 49

CHAPTER THIRTEEN
TB Paul 51

CHAPTER FOURTEEN
Treasure to Trash—Trash to Treasure 53

CHAPTER FIFTEEN
Rabbit Stew *55*

CHAPTER SIXTEEN
Chicken on Sunday *57*

CHAPTER SEVENTEEN
The Price of Pitayas *59*

CHAPTER EIGHTEEN
Who Needs a Doctor? *61*

CHAPTER NINETEEN
Inspiration for Higher Education *71*

CHAPTER TWENTY
Decisions, Decisions *75*

CHAPTER TWENTY-ONE
From Rags to Riches *77*

CHAPTER TWENTY-TWO
Dummy *85*

CHAPTER TWENTY-THREE
Mail Truck Swamper *87*

CHAPTER TWENTY-FOUR
Beating the Rubber Shortage *91*

CHAPTER TWENTY-FIVE
Pulling Up Slack *95*

CHAPTER TWENTY-SIX
Don't Fence Me In *99*

CHAPTER TWENTY-SEVEN
Our Senior Trip *101*

CHAPTER TWENTY-EIGHT
My Last Cattle Drive *105*

CHAPTER TWENTY-NINE
Return to a Remote Canyon Paradise *111*

CELIA HILL FAMILY TREE *113*
CELIA HILL TIMELINE *115*
MAP OF PRESIDIO COUNTY *119*
APPENDIX *121*
ACKNOWLEDGMENTS *125*
ABOUT THE AUTHORS *127*

PREFACE

This collection of stories sets out a first-person account of a family who moved from Memphis, Tennessee, in the late 1800s to Hobart, Oklahoma, and then to Texas, back to Oklahoma and back again to Texas. The Oklahoma stint afforded a memory of Geronimo, so the indecision of the family bore this fruit, if no other.

Through Celia Hill's lens we learn about life in the western part of Texas as she grew to become a competent cowgirl and later a schoolteacher. Except for an epilogue Celia wrote about a homecoming for the people who lived in Terlingua prior to 1946, we have nothing from her own hand about her life after 1945. But an interview by Bob Phillips of *Texas Country Reporter* in 2006 gives us more of her story and interviews with her son, Rusty Hill, fill in more gaps. A transcript of that program, "Show 990," is included in the appendix of this book.

Among the timely and noteworthy information Celia gives to those of us living when the activities along the southern border of the United States show up in every newscast is the fact that Border Patrol agents were part of the fabric of everyday life as early as 1926.

Please note that to preserve the integrity of the journalist's writing, some terminology, common to the time period, may be offensive. Be aware, too, that conventional animal husbandry of the time may not suit modern sensibilities. It was rugged and remote, and yet paradise to many. Enjoy these stories.

Celia Ann Smith. *Courtesy of the family of Celia Hill.*

INTRODUCTION

My favorite road in Texas is in the Big Bend. It stretches south from Marfa around the seldom-traveled Chinati Mountains to the almost ghost town of Ruidosa, Texas. Ranch Road 2810 is not shown on most maps, and there is a good reason why—there isn't much at the end of it other than a few ranches, some abandoned mines, and amazing scenery. It joins a road along the Rio Grande connecting Presidio with both Ruidosa and Candelaria, another wide spot in the road less frequented than Ruidosa. The pavement ends about twenty miles from Marfa, and the road zigs and zags along the sides of the Cretaceous-age peaks and extinct volcanoes and through picturesque Pinto Canyon, with views all the way to Mexico, south of the river.

It is difficult to imagine the possibility of living in this beautiful but desolate place, but in an earlier time a hardy few made a living from growing cotton along the fertile borders of the river and running cattle on immense ranches. During the troubles with Mexico in the early 1900s, the army established outposts along the river to protect the ranchers and other settlers. The fascinating history of these earlier times is recounted in David Keller's comprehensive book on the history of the area, *In the Shadow of the Chinatis: A History of the Canyon in the Big Bend*.

I have driven my four-wheel drive Land Cruiser through the canyon to photograph in Pinto Canyon. By the time I'd pass Chinati Hot Springs and taken time for an hour soak, I would

INTRODUCTION

Picture of storefront with Celia and Rusty. *Courtesy of Bill Wright.*

wind up thirsty and hungry at the little store in Ruidosa. The owner, Celia Hill, was often the only person in sight. All she sold were cold drinks, water, and ready-made sandwiches. Occasionally, her son, Rusty, would be hanging around doing odd jobs for his mom and helping entertain the infrequent visitors.

Several years after we became better acquainted, Celia began to tell me stories about her life in the Big Bend. They were great: full of surprises, amazing discoveries, and a life that would absolutely stun a young woman today. I encouraged her to write it all down. Celia told me that she had already written much of it down and was going to have it published. I offered to help, but she said it wasn't finished.

On a later trip through the canyon, I pulled up to the store, and it was closed. I inquired and found that she had recently died. I wondered what had happened to her journal. I did not know any of her family but her son, Rusty, and I had no idea where he might be living. I inquired around and heard that he

INTRODUCTION

was living in Alpine. We finally made contact in 2018, and again I offered to see if I could get the journal published for the family and the public interested in true stories of old West Texas. Here, Marianne Wood takes over telling the story of my interactions and sets the stage for Celia's life story through her journal and through interviews conducted by others.

BILL WRIGHT

Bill Wright conducted interviews with Celia's son Rusty and daughter Robbie in 2018. He turned the recordings and further research over to me in order to fill out the missing parts of her life. I transcribed the interviews by Jim Glendinning for Marfa Public Radio and by Bob Phillips for *Texas Country Reporter*. These, plus other phone interviews with family members and Internet searches, helped us render additional glimpses into Celia Hill's life after her journal ends. I offer some of these interesting stories to prepare you for Celia's life story in her own words.

Celia left home for Texas Technological College (now Texas Tech University) at age sixteen and stayed one year. There she met and married tall, blue-eyed, husky Walter "Cotton" Sims, a man who became an abusive alcoholic. Walter, a wounded Marine veteran who lost his leg in Guam during WWII, probably met Celia in a math class at Tech. She had two boys with him: Charles Harris and Robert Neal. Celia and Walter's marriage failed, and her aunt "Nanny" Bledsoe with her uncle, Elijah, called "Pim," reared the two boys. We learned from Charles Harris Sims that Pim continued his work in the Big Bend National Park even when Nanny moved to Imperial to teach school. It was in Imperial and at a couple of family Christmases orchestrated by her father that Celia and her boys reconnected for a time.

Celia returned home to Alpine, where she completed her teaching degree in 1951 at Sul Ross State University. Her first teaching job took her to Leakey, Texas. Celia told Jim Glendenning in 2007 that this first teaching job introduced her to seventh-

and eighth-grade students—the age group that "remained my favorite throughout my teaching career." She added that the openness and curiosity of this age group provided no dull moments and made teaching fun. Celia was twenty-one years old.

Before Celia left Sul Ross, Robert Hugh "Bob" Hill, another Sul Ross student, began courting her after an introduction by his twin brother, William "Bill" Hill, who just happened to be married to Celia's sister, Winabeth. Bob had returned to school to work on getting his teaching certificate after serving as a paratrooper in the Korean War. According to Celia's daughter Robbie Hill Burns, he was attracted to Celia because "Mom was gorgeous! What man wouldn't be attracted to a blonde, blue-eyed pretty girl?"

When Celia and Robert married, they moved to Banquete, Texas, where Celia worked for the school district as a bookkeeper. Later they moved to Imperial, Texas, to teach. There they lived in a two-story house that featured an elevator, which was remarkable in those days. The next stop was Glenwood, New Mexico, to teach in a two-room schoolhouse. "She was in one room; he was in the other," Celia's son Rusty told Bill. Robbie noted that these were probably the best years of family life: "We'd travel up to Reserve, New Mexico, and meet up with our parents' friends Wade and Betty McCraley, who had children our age. On weekends we'd go camping and hiking in the Gila Wilderness. Great family time. But then in my sixth-grade year, Dad started drinking heavily. Our family was pretty fragmented from then on."

Next, they moved on to Roswell, where Robert became attracted to another woman. The marriage took another downward turn when he applied for a secret service job and was rejected. As Robbie explained: "All of our lives changed. He (her father) was never physically abusive, but he was emotionally gone. He obtained a grant to study in California at Berkeley, and while there, he took a job in Corona, California." Robert told Celia she could go, too, but she did not want to uproot the family again. Celia stayed in New Mexico and the marriage finally ended upon her discovery that Robert had another girlfriend in California.

Another story Rusty told Bill illustrates just how committed Celia was to her profession of teaching and to parenting her children. Though the family travelled each summer to see extended family in California, in 1968, when Rusty was eight, Celia and the children took "a trip of a lifetime." Starting from home in Roswell in a Chevrolet van with five kids and two dogs, they drove to Oklahoma City to tour the Cowboy Hall of Fame and then drove on to Saint Louis to tour the Budweiser Brewery and famous horse barns plus the Saint Louis Zoo. They saw the world's largest snake at the time "as it had just finished eating a whole freaking cat. The bulge in the snake was as big as I was at the time . . . that was cool," Rusty said. They traveled on to Columbus, Ohio, where relatives Chappy and Billie Moore lived. From enjoying model trains in Columbus, they went on to Philadelphia to see the Liberty Bell and visit Independence Hall. The final destination was Geneseo, New York, where Celia had a grant to attend a seminar in linguistics at the State University of New York. Every weekend of the eight-week seminar, the institute hosted special outings. Faculty accompanied the family. One memory that stuck out for Robbie was when the school's nuns donned '50s-style bathing suits for swimming!

With only three thousand people in the town, the small university reminded Rusty of Sul Ross back home. Inside the school, Rusty and his sisters surprised faculty with their ability to read books off the college bookshelves. Obviously intrigued by the children's accents, faculty members recorded their voices as they read out loud. They became part of a project that demonstrated that language changes from region to region. Rusty illustrates: "You know there's *GARidge* and *gahrodge* . . . subtle differences that exist region to region." The family made trips to the Corning Glass and Kodak plants and made it to Niagara Falls where Rusty noted, "There's more water that goes over that thing than you're [a kid from New Mexico] going to see in your life!" Before

INTRODUCTION

they headed home, they spent four days in New York City, and made it as far as the coastline.

One of Robbie's most memorable things on this trip—besides doing a lot of driving—she was seventeen and the only driver other than her mom—was a lesson in prejudice.

The Hill children had gone to school with all kinds of people, so when trying to get a room for the night in a Virginia motel run by a black person, they had no expectation of racism. In the reception office of the motel Robbie saw the man in the office reach over and hit the "No Vacancy" switch while her mother attempted to secure a room for the night. She told her mother "that's bull crap!" and explained what she'd seen. As they drove out of the motel driveway, the "No Vacancy" sign was lit. Despite the remarks you'll read later, Celia was not racist, but this motel manager was.

Robbie also told us about the fun she had singing and dancing that summer in the musical, "The Most Happy Fella." She also remembered how funny it was when two taxi drivers in NYC got in a fight over who would get to have this family (since it was six people) in their cab. After a bit of back and forth between the men, the first to challenge shoved the family in the taxi and off they went—all in one! They saw the Twin Towers just going up and a NYC garbage strike.

Robert Hill retired from teaching in California in 1979 and moved back to Alpine, Texas, where he opened a liquor store. Living in Alpine and operating a liquor store with his daughter Robbie and son-in-law Dale Burns, Robert drank a lot and eventually could not help run the store. He moved to San Antonio to work with a friend and lived with his daughter Roxie until the time of his death from peritonitis in 1981.

Celia taught in Pecos that year and had a kid pull a knife on her in class. The principal asked her what she was going to do. She made it clear that the student was not coming back to her class! According to Robbie, the principal brought him back to Celia's class after a suspension of only three days, and she refused

INTRODUCTION

to allow him a seat in the classroom. The principal asked, "What am I supposed to do?" Celia's reply: "I don't care." The student did not return to her class, and Celia finished the year before moving to Alpine.

Celia stopped teaching for a while to run the liquor store that Robert had left them. She and Rusty lived in the "gaudy pink house" and together ran "Hill and Dale Liquor" for the Hill family and Robbie's husband, Dale, who was a partner. Rusty said, "Mama came and picked up and actually made a booming business. She tired quickly, though, and desired to return to the teaching field." But before that year ended, she rode her horse from Fort Davis to Alpine—a distance of almost twenty-four miles. The occasion was the Alpine Centennial on April 1, 1982. Robbie told us that she ran the store for her mom that day and it snowed! "The event [Centennial] lasted two days, so Celia and the other riders camped out and came in the next day. Celia rode until she was seventy-five years old."

The fall of 1982 Celia got a teaching job in Terlingua. In the 1980s there were only four rooms for first through eighth grade students. By 1989 Celia was teaching in Anthony, Texas—right on the border. Not liking that position, she accepted the recommendation of a friend to teach in Presidio. "People in Presidio loved her, and she liked it there. It was very close to her home," Rusty said. She began teaching English there in 1991 and retired around 1996. In Presidio Celia met and married her last husband, John Littlejohn, a hunting guide in Ruidosa. He died in 1998. It was he who convinced Celia to purchase the La Junta General Store in Ruidosa.

While teaching in Presidio she began making trips to a ranch above Candelaria. There she met Juanita and Ann Fuentes of what was once called the Fuentes Township—the original name of Ruidosa, Texas. It was in this store that Bill Wright met Celia in the late 1990s.

In the *Texas Country Reporter* episode about her life, Celia admits: "There aren't too many people still living that have the

INTRODUCTION

kind of history that I do. It is about the years we lived in this remote canyon that these stories are told."

In this same episode of the popular travelogue featuring the affable host Bob Phillips, Celia gives Bob a tour of this Ruidosa, Texas, store—the only one "for miles and miles around." Celia's La Junta General Store features "a few snacks ... so that they [the tourists] can keep their stomachs off their backbone," she says, chuckling. Since the nearest Walmart is in Chihuahua City, Mexico (165 miles), or Odessa, Texas, USA (221 miles), it's a good thing she was there. Beanie Weenies, Spam, and Vienna Sausages, along with peanut butter, foil-packaged tuna, and an assortment of drinks are shown on a shelf. The store also serves as a museum, and Celia proudly showed Bob the last mohair blanket that was made in Mexico from goats on her family's ranch.

Rusty remarked that the store opened selling mainly beer and ice cream, but "because so many people would drive up to Hot Springs and not realize there was not any food, Mom got to carrying more stuff ... $45 to $50 picnic packs that included a can of vegetables, a can of fruit, and a couple of sodas, plus ... firewood."

To illustrate how little traffic she saw, Rusty told how they would "sit on the porch at eleven o'clock until about 1:00 pm, and if there were five cars, well, there's a lot of traffic!"

As Celia told Jim Glendenning, the appeal of living on the frontier was the tranquility. "Even though the Border Patrol tell us we have terrorists, I don't lie awake at night [chuckling] in fear at all. There are no trucks, no trains going by, and not very many dogs that are barking all night."

And to the people who came to her store who asked if she'd lived there all her life she liked to say, "Not quite!"

Quite a life. Thank you, Celia, for writing down what you could and for sharing much of the rest of it with Jim and Bob and Bill.

MARIANNE WOOD

☞ CELIA HILL'S JOURNAL ☜
INTRODUCTION

On October 29 to 31, 2004, a homecoming for all people who had lived in the area prior to 1946 was held in Terlingua. This was a community effort coordinated by Cynta De Narvaes. A small museum with pictures from 1930s and other artifacts was set up in one room of the old store building. A video of "Life in Terlingua" was available for viewing.

Approximately four hundred people showed up for this event. I met Elizabeth (Betty) Cartledge Rogers of Buda, Texas, daughter of Robert Cartledge. We enjoyed reminiscing. Our fathers had enjoyed going to ballgames in later years when they both lived in Austin, Texas. Also, I met Patricia Rios, whose aunt Nestora had been my babysitter and whose uncles, Alberto and Norberto Rios, had both worked for Daddy in the mines at Fresno. Juan Miranda, whose father and uncles had worked in the Fresno Mines, was there, too. Juan lives in Presidio now. Juan's sister attended the homecoming.

Juan told us the story of his uncles and the draft board. After WWII was declared and most of the able-bodied men were drafted, Daddy was able to get exemptions for some of the men who worked the mines because mercury was a premium commodity. He told them that they must not miss a day of work other than for illness. One weekend a friend of theirs got married in Carlsbad, New Mexico, and they went on three-day drinking binge. When

INTRODUCTION

they came back to work, a representative of the draft board was there waiting for them, and they were immediately inducted into the army.

About mid-morning of October 9, 2005, a lady, Mary Hutchinson, came into my store in Ruidosa from Hawkins, Texas. She told me that her grandparents, Gus and Maude Bogle, had lived at Sauceda, which is now headquarters for the Big Bend Ranch State Park. She had come here to scatter her grandmother's ashes.

I then told her that I had barely remembered being neighbors with her grandparents. My father had bought a horse from her grandfather, which my mother always rode. They named the horse Gus. Her grandfather had saved me from drowning one afternoon at our swimming hole. I was just a toddler and had jumped into the tank to swim like the other children. Gus heard the thrashing in the water and reached down to pick me up out of the water. The world gets smaller the longer I am a part of it.

Celia's daughter, Robbie, remembers that she and her family would meet in the park basin (Big Bend) every summer and make a trip to see how things were progressing. "Granddad always said that if we showed we were prospecting, we'd never lose our mineral rights." The company cheated Granddad on the lease the second time around. The lease agreement called for a monthly payment of $1,500 per month, but when the second lease was signed, the lessor moved the decimal point and paid him $150 per month.

☞ CELIA HILL'S JOURNAL ☜
PROLOGUE

William Oliver Smith and Adecia Ann Walker were married in 1886 in Memphis, Tennessee. An infant son born in 1886 died in 1887, and another son, Sam Less, was born in 1888 and died at the age of two months. Their daughter, Eady Enon, was born in 1889. A son, Ollie, was born in 1892 and died in 1894 from eating raw macaroni. And Harris Seymour was born on October 5, 1894.

W. O. and Adecia piled all of their household goods and furniture into a covered wagon and left Memphis, Tennessee, in 1894, when Harris was a baby. They headed west to seek their fortune and a dry climate where W. O.'s health would improve. They settled in Hobart, Oklahoma, for a short time before moving to Dawson, Texas, a small town about seventy-five miles south of Dallas, where a fifth child, Elizabeth, was born on September 10, 1895.

They moved back to Oklahoma to Lone Wolf, where W. O. was in the mercantile business and traded with the Indians. Harris could remember sitting on Geronimo's knee when he was a small boy. Shortly thereafter they decided to move back to Texas, only farther west than Dawson.

W. O. and Harris arrived in Alpine in 1901 riding in a boxcar with a Jersey milk cow. Harris was wearing a double-breasted suit. Underneath one lapel was a note: "To Whom It May Concern"

PROLOGUE

Smith House—first frame home in Alpine. *Courtesy of the family of Celia Hill.*

giving instructions what to do with this young boy if something happened to his father. The rest of the family soon joined them. W. O. proceeded to build the first frame house in the community. He had a small ranch in the neighborhood of Goat Mountain—southeast of Paisano Pass. Adecia became the first kindergarten teacher in Alpine. Classes were held in what is now called the Sunshine House.

Harris was the only boy in the 1912 graduating class of Alpine High School. After graduation, he went to El Paso to seek his fortune. One cold morning, while delivering milk for a dairy, he received his calling for higher education.

He went to San Marcos, where he enrolled in Southwest Texas Normal School. It was there that he met his future bride, Winnie Donald. After receiving an associate degree, he taught school in Kingsville approximately six months before he was called into the service for World War I. He was stationed at Camp Leon Springs near San Antonio as a training officer. Harris and Winnie were married in Brookshire, Texas, on December 20, 1917.

PROLOGUE

Winnie was one of a set of twin girls, Winnie and Willie, born to William Franklin Donald and Celestia Greer of Brookshire, Texas, on November 16, 1898. A third child, Warren Franklin "Jack" Donald, was born August 4, 1906.

William Franklin Donald was born on May 15, 1862, in Fairfield, Virginia. Being one of ten children, he left home at the age of fifteen. He and two brothers, Sydney and Warren, struck out for California. They arrived in Kyle, Texas, in November of 1881. W. F. stayed in Kyle with a cousin, Mary Hartson, while the other two continued their journey west. Mary Hartson was the postmistress in Kyle. She was one of the first postmistresses in the United States.

While living in Kyle, W. F. took part in several cattle drives following the Chisholm Trail from the grasslands of Texas to Kansas City, Kansas. On one such excursion, marauding Indians who were scalp hunters chased the drovers, who managed to escape. W. F. eventually migrated to Brookshire, where he opened a livery stable. He furnished horses and wagons to drummers who peddled their wares in a twenty-mile radius. W. F. soon made the acquaintance of Celestia Greer who worked at the Gladys Hotel, which was owned and operated by her sister, Mary.

Celestia (nicknamed Lelly) was born July 12, 1874. She grew up on a farm near Pattison, Texas, north of Brookshire.

W. F. Donald and Celestia Greer were married in 1896. They went through some hard times. The storm of 1900 that destroyed Galveston and took so many lives also destroyed the W. F. Donald Hardware Store.

Through the years W. F. became quite successful as a merchant. He also acquired considerable land holdings and had several sharecroppers working on his land. I never remember Grandma Lelly referring to W. F. as anyone but "Mr. Donald." We called him "Daddy Donald." Lelly never had to lift her hand to any menial tasks after she married. All work was to be done by "darkies." Every day, Tildy, the Negro cook, would go across the street to the store and Mr. Donald would select what he wanted for lunch. Tildy could not read; therefore, she looked at the pictures on the labels and proceeded accordingly.

Prior to the coming of air conditioning, oscillating fans were used for cooling. A large oscillating fan was used to cool most of the group of people eating at the dining room table. A large palm fan being waved up and down by a grandson of Tildy also cooled Mr. Donald. There was no conversation during the meal.

Mr. Donald was a large man who reminded me of Lionel Barrymore who starred in the *Littlest Colonel* series of movies with Shirley Temple. He always wore light grey or light blue pinstriped suits and Panama straw hats. The summer hats had a wider brim than the winter ones. He was always very proper.

During the summers it was customary for us to spend six weeks with my grandparents in Brookshire at the same time that my Aunt Billie would come home for a visit from Ohio. Most of the time we rode the Southern Pacific train from Alpine to Rosenburg, where my Uncle Jack would pick us up and take us on to Brookshire. One summer we rode to Austin with the Clifford Caseys, and Uncle Jack picked us up there.

I always thought that Mama would let us go barefoot at least one day where Daddy Donald could see us, because if he ever caught us barefooted, he would immediately march us up the street and around the corner to "Dan Six Bits' Dry Goods" store, where we would be fitted with socks and shoes. Only the darkies went barefooted! Many things in Dan's store were priced to end in seventy-five cents, thus the moniker Dan Six Bits'.

Every Saturday night, Daddy Donald would sit out on the little screened-in porch smoking his cigar and listening to *Amos and Andy*. How he enjoyed that program! What Mr. Donald lacked in formal education, he made up for by reading and listening to people.

While Harris was stationed at Camp Leon Springs, Winnie made blankets from woolen "tails" that were cut off the army men's coats after the styles changed.

After the end of the war, they moved out to New Mexico.

PROLOGUE

They lived near Ruidoso on the slopes of Monjeau. They later settled in El Paso, where Winnie taught school and Harris sold real estate. His sister, Enon, was living there also.

Their first child Winabeth was born May 10, 1922. The following year the family moved to Oak Creek on the west side, at the foot of the window [a hiking trail].[1] This was a totally new experience for Winnie, having been reared on a ranch. Harris brought Hereford cattle and the first registered Angora goats to the Big Bend.

The house in Oak Creek was a two-story prefab home built by Sears, Roebuck and Company. It shipped by train on a flat car to Marathon, Texas, to the Rooney family. They in turn moved it by wagon to Nine Point Mesa about halfway between Marathon and the Chisos Mountains. The house was later moved to Oak Creek. The Rooneys sold the ranch to Charlie Burnham, father of Evelyn Burnham Fulcher. In 1923, Charlie sold the ranch to Harris Smith.

The Smiths' second child, Willeen, was born on January 2, 1926, in Brookshire, Texas, and their third child, Celia Ann, was born in Alpine on May 25, 1928. The two-story, red brick building on the corner of US 67/90 and Eleventh Street was the community hospital at this time. I was born in the southeastern corner room on the second floor. This building is now Mike Barclay's law office.

The Smiths sold out to Homer Wilson in 1929 and moved over to Fresno Canyon a few miles north of Lajitas. Harris bought this ranch from James L. Crawford, brother to Hallie Crawford Stillwell. It is about the years that we lived in this remote canyon paradise that these stories are told.

---

1 *The Window Trail is one of the most popular hikes in Big Bend. It starts near the Chisos Mountain Lodge and descends to a narrow opening in the rim of rock that creates the Chisos Basin. It is the sole exit point for water runoff out of the basin, so obviously you would not want to be near the Window at times of heavy rain.* http://www.texashiking.com/Locations/ShowLocation.aspx?LocationID=140.

☞ CELIA HILL'S JOURNAL ☜
CHAPTER ONE
Life in Terlingua

Get There or Bust. *Courtesy of the family of Celia Hill.*

Mama started teaching school in Terlingua in 1930 for a salary of $100 per month. Out of this sum she sent her twin sister in Ohio $15 per month, maintained the household, and helped Daddy with the expenditures of the ranch in Fresno Canyon.

Winabeth attended school in Terlingua from first through eighth grades. Willeen attended school in Study Butte where our aunt, Elizabeth Weaver, was her teacher. I stayed at home with a babysitter/housekeeper by the name of Nestora Rios, who

CHAPTER ONE

was the daughter of a neighboring rancher, Manuel Rios. Fortunately, when I was learning to talk, I also learned Spanish, since Nestora spoke no English. This was a distinct advantage to me later in life.

By the time I was five years old, I thought I was too big to take a nap every day after lunch. I would much rather be hiking around over the hills or riding horseback. Behind the Terlingua store a large compound of horses, mules, and burros were corralled. These animals were used to pull freight wagons from Terlingua to Alpine and back. They hauled all of the provisions for the store and the mines as well as carried the mail. Under normal circumstances, it took two weeks to make the round trip. They hauled flasks of mercury from the mines to the railhead in Alpine.

I learned that Mr. Robert Cartledge, who was the store manager, kept a very gentle horse in the compound behind the store. He would let me ride the horse any time I wanted, or should I say, any time I had permission. My biggest problem was getting from our house all the way to the wagon yard without being caught. Our house was at the end of the road going north. The school was between the store and our house. Invariably one or two of mama's students would be watching out the window and would see me as I tried to sneak from one creosote bush to another. I think she gave them "an A for the day" if they spotted me, and then reported back to her. I can see her to this day leaning out the window and calling to me to go back to the house because it was too hot to be out in the sun.

On one such occasion when I managed to make my getaway, my friend Betty Waters and I rode double over to Rainbow Mine and back. On the way home we rode beneath an overhanging mesquite limb. The horse stepped up a ledge just as we rode beneath a branch. She didn't duck enough and got brushed off the back of the horse. Luckily, she was not injured. She and I spent many happy hours together riding over hills.

Another of my friends was Isaac Hernandez, whose father was the town barber after he got off work from the mine. One spring afternoon I went down to see Isaac to discover that either he or one of his friends had some new puppies. I took one home with me, to the utter dismay of my mother. She wouldn't allow ANY pets in the house. The puppy was too small, however, to leave outside until he got older. I was too small to take care of it during the night; consequently, that duty fell to the older girls. The puppy was solid black except for one small white spot on his chest. I named him Sir Wolf Prince Rover Smith, which was soon shortened to Prince Rover or Poochie. As soon as possible we took him over to the ranch in Fresno Canyon.

When Prince Rover was about three months old, Edwin Fowlkes rode horseback from his ranch at Sauceda over to see us, which he was wont to do on a Sunday. He took it upon himself to cut the puppy's tail off. I was mortified! The puppy recovered before I did. I never liked that man from that day on.

These were the days of prohibition. One day a Mexican man had come into the community to sell some of his contraband. He was the first person intercepted on the south side of town by a local law enforcement officer. He was trying to escape through the arroyo, which ran below our house to the west. As the outlaw came up out of the arroyo in a dead run, the deputy shot the horse out from under him. I was in total awe as I watched them handcuff the outlaw, take the saddle off the horse, and take the prisoner to jail. They passed right by our house. After school was out, it was a big attraction to play "double dog dare" to see who would run closest to the dead horse.

☞ CELIA HILL'S JOURNAL ☜
CHAPTER TWO
Rare Commodities

Ice was a rare commodity. We had one of the wooden ice boxes with a tin compartment for a block of ice and wire shelves through which the air would flow to keep foods cool. An old Mexican man named Santiago would come around once or twice week in a wagon drawn by mules with a wagon full of two hundred-pound blocks of ice. He cut the large blocks into fifty-pound blocks of ice and sold them to the people. I can remember the thrill of going out to meet Santiago. As he would saw the larger blocks into smaller pieces, we would hold our hands cupped to get the shavings. It was just like having a snow cone, which became popular many years later.

Another treat would be to eat ice while taking a hot bath. Mama loved to eat ice. Willeen and I were small enough to both fit into a #3 washtub. Water would be heated in kettles on the stove and then added to cold water in the washtub. While we were scrubbing up in the washtub, Mama would chip ice off the big block in the icebox and hand it to us to eat.

Meat was also a rare commodity. About twice a month, on Fridays, Walter Fulcher, who was a local rancher, would come around in his truck with freshly butchered beef that he sold to patrons in Terlingua and Study Butte. He would slice off steaks or roasts to order and sell trimmings that we would grind into hamburger.

CHAPTER TWO

House at Oak Creek Big Bend National Park, 1926. *Courtesy of the family of Celia Hill.*

I can remember several times that I asked to go with him to Study Butte. I pretended that I was running away from home. We would arrive in Study Butte, where my aunt Elizabeth Weaver was a teacher, just before dismissal time. She would send word back with Mr. Fulcher that she would bring me home later in the day. I got to play with my sister Willeen, who was going to school there. I missed her during the week when I had to stay home alone with the housekeeper, Nestora Rios.

Harris and Celia (in the back), and Willeen and Winabeth. *Courtesy of the family of Celia Hill.*

Willeen, Celia, and Winabeth. *Courtesy of the family of Celia Hill.*

Willeen, Celia, and Winabeth Smith, 1930. *Courtesy of the family of Celia Hill.*

Celia and Willeen. *Courtesy of the family of Celia Hill.*

Harris with Celia, age five, in Fresno Canyon. *Courtesy of the family of Celia Hill.*

☞ CELIA HILL'S JOURNAL ☜
CHAPTER THREE
Seven in One

Shortly after moving to Fresno Canyon, Daddy discovered that the ranch was overrun with wild burros. This was not good because they ate valuable grass for the cattle and goats. He decided to dispatch most of them.

One afternoon Daddy and Lige Bledsoe, a friend of our aunt Elizabeth, were out riding around in a truck when they came upon a small herd of burros. They had a 30-30 rifle with them and Lige decided to take a shot at one of the burros.

The herd had bunched up on a V-shaped piece of land between two arroyos. Lige fired a shot at one of the burros and the shot went through his neck and into the burro standing behind him, killing him also. Three of the burros that were out on the point of land were shoved over the brink of the arroyo in the melee and broke their necks. One died when it was kicked in the head and another when its back was broken. Daddy and Lige came in telling how Lige had killed seven burros with one shot!

☞ CELIA HILL'S JOURNAL ☜
CHAPTER FOUR
Johnson's Ranch

The first Easter that I can remember was spent at the Elmo Johnson Ranch on the south side of the Chisos Mountains. The Johnsons hosted fish fries during the years that we lived in Terlingua. All of the Anglo families from both sides of the Chisos Mountains and those who lived between there and Marathon would get together and camp out for the weekend. Those families I remember were Bill Burchams, Bill Coopers, Leroy Stones from Hovey, Greens, Charlie Burnhams, Waddy Burnhams, Homer Wilson, Sam Nails, Edd Babb, Robert Cartledge, Wayne Cartledge, and I am sure there were others.

All the families brought something to share with everyone else. Right after the Mexican Revolution, Elmo was still having trouble with some of the Mexicans from across the Rio Grande. A very primitive landing strip near the ranch was cleared for emergency use by the US Air Force as a refueling station while patrolling the border between Del Rio and El Paso, providing security to the ranchers.

After experiencing the hospitality of the Johnsons and having eaten Mrs. Johnson's cooking, several of the pilots would make it a point to have an "emergency" requiring an overnight stay. It was on one of those occasions when a fish fry was being held and several pilots were experiencing difficulties requiring emergency landings that I saw my first airplane. Early in the

CHAPTER FOUR

day the pilots were giving free rides to anyone who wanted to take one.

My mother was so frightened by these contraptions that she made my father promise never to ride in one. She threatened to cut her hair if he ever did. Mama had beautiful long hair down to her waist. True to his word, he never rode in a plane until years after she passed away. This was when he flew to Ohio to see Mama's twin sister and her husband, who had been a very good friend of Daddy's back in school in San Marcos. While he was there, they were involved in a car accident. Daddy broke his hip and was hospitalized for a couple of months. He always said that he was getting his just deserts for breaking his promise to Mama.

☞ CELIA HILL'S JOURNAL ☜
CHAPTER FIVE
Whistle While You Work

Many a summer morning I would awaken to the sound of mother whistling as she worked in the garden. Suddenly the tune would change, and it would be followed by a call, "Winabeth, Willeen, Celia, bring a bucket or a pan and come help me." She would already have several containers full of vegetables.

Our garden was approximately two acres in size, arranged in terraces located on the south side of the house between the house and corrals. The upper terrace contained the smaller produce: bush green beans, tomatoes, squash, peppers, cucumbers, onions, and lettuce. The second terrace contained okra, corn, and pole green beans. The third terrace was where the cantaloupes and watermelons grew.

Milk, butter and eggs, and the salad vegetables were kept in a cooler that consisted of metal rack of shelves located in an open breezeway almost the size of a door. The upper shelf had a two-inch rim that held water. A drip system, connected to the outside water line, brought cool water from the spring. The upper edge of a lightweight canvas sheet was tucked into this tray of water while the sheet was wrapped around the rack and hung down into another catchment tray at the bottom. The water wicked down the sheet. The air blowing through the breezeway around this wet canvas acted as an evaporative cooler. Excess water at

CHAPTER FIVE

the bottom was drained off outside and watered hollyhocks near an orange tree. Some of the vegetables, such as squash, okra, tomatoes, corn, and green beans would be canned.

On the north side of the house we had a sizeable orchard containing three different varieties of peaches—Elberta, White Clingstone, and also a White Freestone. There were a couple apricot trees in the yard, along with a huge fig tree. In front of the house were two plum trees and several pecan trees. Peaches, apricots, plums, and figs would be preserved. Three large orange trees were on the south side of the house. We even canned the juice from one of the orange trees that had frozen. When it came back out, the fruit was too sour to eat, but the juice mixed with other fruit juice made good fruit punch.

Once or twice a summer we would make the trip over the mesa to the old Madrid Ranch. I grew up believing that this was the site of an old mission. In later years, I was told by Enrique Madrid of Redford that it was actually the site of his great-grandfather's ranch. We climbed up over the steep winding trails across the mesa then down into Madrid Canyon [Canyon Primera], taking along two or three burros loaded with angarillas [Mexican panniers] containing fifty-pound "Mrs. Tucker's" lard cans. After filling our cans with figs, we would picnic in the shade of the cottonwood and ash trees that grew beside the creek, wading in the cool, crystal-clear water of the creek—sometimes chasing a water snake up the creek.

Before we left for home, we always checked the pomegranate trees. These would ripen in August and early September. I have never had such sweet-tasting pomegranates. They were such a deep red color. I could understand why in later years, as I studied literature, I learned that pomegranates were "food for the gods."

In the kitchen we girls took turns watching the pressure cooker so that a steady temperature would be maintained. We had to keep feeding the wood stove just the right amount of fuel for this. I recall how hot it would get in the kitchen! But those vegetables and fruits tasted oh, so good when we were in Alpine during the winter going to school.

Canning sessions would occasionally bring company. When the Wilsons bought Oak Creek, Mrs. (Bergine) Wilson was a novice to life on a ranch in such an isolated area. She was eager to learn how to do the many chores, however, and Bergine came to Mama for instructions in how to preserve fruit and can vegetables. We looked forward to these times because we enjoyed having her daughter, Patricia, to play with. Not only did the Wilsons come to Fresno Canyon, but we would go to Oak Creek when fruit was ripe over there. After work was done, we would either hike or ride horseback to Cattail Falls, where we would go swimming in the pool below the falls. This water would compare to Barton Springs for coldness, so we didn't stay in very long. On several occasions, we were joined by Julia Nail [Moss] who lived down the road a piece from Oak Creek. We would sometimes ride over to her house for a visit. Daddy had bought Pinochle, a popular card game in those days, from Julie's father.

It was during these canning sessions of watching the pressure cooker that we did a lot reading. I can remember learning to read from the cereal boxes and what few packaged foods that we used. In those days, the *Saturday Evening Post* and *Life* magazines were an important part of our lives. Occasionally, the *Saturday Evening Post* published stories in serial format. A big decision had to be made as to whether we read each week's issue as it arrived or whether we waited until we had the whole story. We usually got mail from Terlingua only once or twice a month because it took up all of one day to drive the twenty-two miles over and back. Unless it rained and the road had to be worked, then it took longer. The whole family were avid readers. Mother and Daddy saw that we were supplied with a bounty of good literature.

To this day, I find myself emulating my mother by whistling as I work in my garden, where I derive a great deal of pleasure. I also enjoy a good book to read as I sit in the shade of a tree or on a patio while I'm watering the yard.

☞ CELIA HILL'S JOURNAL ☜
CHAPTER SIX
The Spring

O ur water came from a spring up in the canyon to the west of the house. The entire pipeline was above ground. In all eighteen years that we lived on the ranch, the water in the pipes froze and burst only once. The water was tested by the state periodically. Always, when the analysis came back, Daddy would tell us "it's like Ivory Soap: 99 to 100 percent pure."

Up near the head of the spring was a concrete spring box where the water collected and then ran through a pipe by gravity flow down the mountain to another catchment box. When it rained and the spring canyon would run, we would have to go up and clean the silt out of the *pilas*. It was always a good place to take visitors for a hike. The lower pools provided a place for a refreshing dip on a hot day. The canyon walls were covered with columbine and maidenhair ferns. There was nearly always a patch or two of poison ivy to beware of, too.

The water from the spring was piped into the house. It also fed into a dirt tank with a rocked-in dam that Daddy had built in a small cul-de-sac across the road from the house. This tank provided water for irrigating the garden and orchard, as well as a place for us to swim in the late evenings. The rule was that as soon as the sun went behind the mountain and the tank was in the shadows, we could go in swimming. I can remember on a hot summer afternoon we would get into our swimsuits and

CHAPTER SIX

sit on the front porch while we waited and watched for the shadows.

When we had guests, a swim tank was always a refreshing way to end a fun-filled day of riding horseback or hunting arrowheads. Occasionally we would take the horses swimming with us. We would ride them bareback out on the concrete dam and jump off into the cool water. They also enjoyed the refreshing water after a hard day's ride in the sun.

☞ CELIA HILL'S JOURNAL ☜
CHAPTER SEVEN
Politics

Since we lived in the far southern end of Presidio County, and we were the last ones after the road dropped off the mesa into Fresno Canyon, we didn't have the luxury of a nice graded road all the time. The county maintainer worked the road at least once every two to three years, depending on whether or not the commissioner wanted to be re-elected. If the incumbent wanted to keep his position, he would always see that the road was worked, and he would come down and ask for Mama and Daddy's vote. Of course, if the challenger for the position won, he would see that the road was worked early into his term of office and promised to keep it maintained. Most of the maintenance was done with pick and shovel by Mexican workers and Daddy. Sometimes we girls even contributed to the project.

We always looked forward to election time. The polling place was in the Casa Piedra School, which was thirty-five miles from our house. Mama would usually fry up some chicken and make potato salad. We would take fresh produce from the garden and maybe a cake or cookies. All of the ranchers from the surrounding area would meet in Casa Piedra. The assembly included P. A. Jackson, the Gus Bogle family from Sauceda, the Jack Rawls family, the Elliots, and the Smiths to name a few.

The children all gathered under the cottonwood trees in Alamito Creek and played in the water while the adults were

CHAPTER SEVEN

visiting, discussing the weather, the price of cattle, or the price of mohair. When it was time for lunch, tables would be made consisting of long planks resting on sawhorses in the shade of the cottonwood trees along the bank of the creek. All the ladies would set out what they had brought us to eat. What a feast we had! We would stay until the ballots were counted for the local box so that everyone would at least know who our new commissioner would be. The results for the rest of the elected officials sometimes would not reach us for several weeks or a month.

☞ CELIA HILL'S JOURNAL ☜
CHAPTER EIGHT
Pink Glass—Russo

Two of our most memorable visitors were an old man and his daughter from Russia. They arrived at the ranch late one evening in an old wooden wagon drawn by two very worn-out mules. They were on their way to California but had made a wrong turn somewhere to end up in South Brewster and Presidio Counties. They camped under the cottonwood trees for several days to rest up. During the course of their recovery, the old man (Daddy called him "Russo") and Daddy entered into negotiations to trade the wagon and mules for two good saddle horses complete with the trappings. Finally, the day of the departure arrived. Father and daughter had repacked, and with much discussion had decided what they could put into saddlebags and feasibly carry with them.

Besides the wagon and mules, we acquired some unusual pink glass dishes along with other odds and ends of household goods. For years we kept those pink glass dishes with our good china. Since there was a setting of only four of each piece, we did not use them often. They were among the items I inherited after my mother passed away. And they have since been handed down to my granddaughter Elizabeth Klinksiek (Palfino).

☞ CELIA HILL'S JOURNAL ☜
CHAPTER NINE
The Feed Bin and Border Patrol

B
eing so close to the Mexican border, Daddy worked illegal Mexicans on the ranch like all other ranchers in the area. No white man would come so far from Alpine or Marfa and stay two months or more at the time. They wanted to go to town every weekend, which was impossible. The Border Patrol had agents in the Big Bend as early as 1926. Then, as now, they made regular patrols out of Marfa down on the river. Several times they would encounter a goat herder out in the field. He was immediately arrested and taken to La Tuna near El Paso for six months. It might be several days before Daddy would discover the flock of one thousand goats wandering aimlessly over the hills without a herder and several months before we saw the worker again. This created feelings of animosity.

From the ranch house, which was situated in Fresno Canyon, it was quite easy to hear a car from a mile or more away. Late one evening Daddy and the worker, Moises Lujan, from Mulatto, Chihuahua, were down at the corral milking. Moises stayed at the house full-time. They heard a car coming up the canyon and then it stopped. They heard the car door slam, which put them on alert. It was easy to see down the creek bed for a quarter mile or more. When they first saw someone walking up the creek, Moises went into the barn and climbed into one of the wooden feed bins that held bran for the milk cows.

CHAPTER NINE

The Border Patrolman, who was dressed in plain khaki clothes, came up to the corral and addressed Daddy, "Good evening, Harris, you down here milking all by yourself?"

Daddy recognized the man as Shelly Barnes. "Yes, I'm down here all alone," Daddy replied.

As they talked, they moved into the barn because the Border Patrol officer wanted to check it out. Daddy hiked one hip and sat on top of the feed bin where Moises was hiding, and Shelly sat on another. He told Daddy that his car had broken down a little ways down the canyon. Then Daddy looked him in the eye and said, "Shelly, you don't have to lie to me. I know you are a Border Patrol agent and you're looking for illegals, but you can very well see that I don't have anyone working for me." That pretty much ended the investigation. I never knew how Moises could lie so still on that bran without sneezing.

☞ CELIA HILL'S JOURNAL ☜
CHAPTER TEN
Predator Control

When I was about ten years old, we had a government trapper named "Shorty" working on our ranch. It was during the Thanksgiving holidays, when furs were always thicker and filled out more in the winter months. He allowed me to go with him one day when he was running traps west of the old Madrid ranch on the backside of our ranch. There was a badger caught in one of the traps. He was a beautiful animal but was most ferocious. Later in school, he learned that a badger, pound for pound, is one of the most ferocious animals in North America. I'll never forget the size of his claws!

It was on this trip that I learned to respect my horse's back feet. I had ridden him only a few times the previous summer. Daddy had already warned me of Calcitin's habit of kicking, and the danger involved. The ranch hands had ridden him several times and felt it was safe for me to ride him, taking due precautions.

Shorty and I had ground-hitched our horses while he took care of the badger. We were ready to head back to the ranch. Both horses had moved into a mesquite bush to grab a few bites of green grass growing under the branches. Shorty caught his horse with no trouble. The reins from my horse were dragging behind him, but there was no way to approach him from the front. I reached down to grab the reins, and the horse just caught

CHAPTER TEN

a glimpse of movement. He whirled around and let fly with both hind feet. Fortunately, as he whirled, I dodged to one side and felt only the whoosh of air from his feet as they came flying toward me. It almost scared Shorty to death—he just knew he was a goner.

Coyotes and eagles were two predators that plagued the ranches of West Texas, particularly during spring, when the baby lambs and calves were coming on. It was always a debate whether to use poison or traps to eliminate these nuisances. That is, until Mr. John Casparis came to Alpine and started his flying service. J. O. Casparis was noted for his ability to shoot eagles out of the sky while hunting the bluffs and crags of the Davis Mountains. The ranchers would also pool together and hire Mr. Casparis to make a coyote drive.

It was in the spring of 1945 that I was invited to take part in a coyote drive in the Hovey area. The Leroy Stones invited me out to their ranch for a weekend. Ann Stone picked me up in Alpine as soon as school was out on a Friday afternoon. The Stones had joined the Joe Haiters and some other ranchers of that area to make a drive.

We started early Saturday morning shortly after sunup. There must have been close to twenty riders stretched along a line spaced fifty to seventy-five yards apart. Mr. Casparis, in his airplane, would make a sweep along the line in one direction, then double back in the opposite direction. When he sighted a coyote, he would cut the motor of his plane to alert the nearest rider. About every other rider was armed with a 30-30 rifle. The rider would bear down in a hard run upon the coyote to kill it. Six coyotes were bagged that day; three right in front of me.

☞ CELIA HILL'S JOURNAL ☜
CHAPTER ELEVEN
When the Dogs Bark

During the years of 1930–1934, when mother was teaching in Terlingua, several times a year we would host weekend parties when friends from Study Butte, Terlingua, Alpine, and as far away as Hovey would come down for the weekend. Some of them would arrive on Friday afternoon, others on Saturday, and they would stay until Sunday. Some would go swimming in the tank while others went horseback riding. At night, the children would play "kick the can" or "hide and go seek." The adults played "Pinochle," "Dominoes," or "Forty-two."

During the heat of the day, the young people also would play card games. Some of the games played were "Go Fish," "Battle," "Seven-Up," "Flinch," and "Spoons." Sometimes the goat herders would all come in for provisions. As they sat around their campfire visiting, they would sing songs accompanied by an accordion or an old guitar. They sang "Cielito Lindo," "Las Palomas," "Rancho Grande," "La Cucaracha," and other songs. I can remember going to sleep on several occasions being serenaded by these workers.

All day Saturday would be spent barbecuing a goat, frying fresh catfish, making potato salad, cooking other vegetables from the garden, and making fresh green salad. The largest catfish Daddy ever caught on a trotline weighed sixty pounds. When it was being fried, some of the pieces of meat "jumped" out of the

Winnie (Donald) Smith and Harris Smith. *Courtesy of the family of Celia Hill.*

Smith and Focht children swimming in the Fresno Swim Tank. *Courtesy of the family of Celia Hill.*

skillet. Nestora, the Mexican girl who was helping, ran out of the kitchen and wouldn't go back until all of the fish had been cooked. For dessert, we nearly always made ice cream, sometimes using fresh peaches from the orchard or fresh pitayas. The ice would be brought down from Alpine in two-hundred pound blocks.

The younger children were allowed to sit on the ice cream freezer while the older ones or an adult turned the crank. The children would be rewarded with the dasher from the freezer after an adult had duly scraped it off. It was on one such occasion that the partying had gone on until the wee hours. The dogs began barking furiously down the corrals. The men, after a great deal of discussion, decided that the dogs had cornered a skunk down by the barn, and that it was unnecessary to check it out. The next morning, however, when the "troops" went down to go for a horseback ride, there were only two saddles on the racks—an old McClellan split-seated saddle and a big wooden-horned charro

CHAPTER ELEVEN

saddle. Robbers had cleaned all others out during the night. The trail where cinches, girth straps, and stirrups had been dragged through the corrals, across the creek and up a very steep mountain was plain to see. To this day, I listen to the tone of the dogs' barking to determine whether or not it is worth investigating.

☞ CELIA HILL'S JOURNAL ☜
CHAPTER TWELVE
Wash Day Blues

Like every other family, the day arrived when we had to make a decision and either do laundry or stay in bed. We elected to do laundry. The wash shed at the ranch was located about thirty feet out the kitchen door under a large pecan tree. Off to one side was a fire pit where a fire was started early in the morning. A large cast iron wash pot was set over the coals and filled with water. The sheets and linens, white clothes, then light colored, and finally jeans would be put in the kettle to boil for about thirty minutes. They were lifted out on a broom handle into a tub in which they carried to a washing machine—a Maytag wringer model that was powered by a gasoline motor. When we moved to Alpine for the school year, the gasoline motor was taken off and replaced by an electric motor.

Occasionally, if the weather happened to be extremely hot and there was not much breeze, I can remember the exhaust from the motor would overcome Mama. She would have to go inside and lie down for a while. When that happened, Winabeth was left to run the machine. Willeen and I would take turns scrubbing socks and underwear on a rub board. I used that same machine until 1955 and got my braids in the wringer only one time.

Nestora and Winabeth would do ironing with a gasoline iron. Willeen and I learned to iron with flat irons heated on the

CHAPTER TWELVE

wood stove. We ironed handkerchiefs, boxer shorts, dish towels, and pillowcases. More than one would turn up with a scorched spot from an iron that was too hot.

☞ CELIA HILL'S JOURNAL ☜
CHAPTER THIRTEEN
TB Paul

Daddy was the administrator of the Public Works Administration in Alpine in 1935. Under his supervision, the rock retaining wall around the grounds of Sul Ross State University, the original museum, and the rock cottages for married couples were all constructed. The retaining wall has been modified, and all of the cottages have been dismantled.

One day, a very tall, emaciated man named Paul stopped by Daddy's office. He was looking for work of any kind. He was from somewhere back east where he had contracted tuberculosis and was seeking a dry climate where he might recuperate. Daddy had a heart of gold and took in nearly every stray that needed a friend, be it man or beast. It was in the spring of the year. Daddy offered to take Paul to the ranch where he was assigned the task of keeping the weeds out of the garden and the wood box full of wood. He was out in the air and sunshine most of the day but was allowed to rest when he felt the need.

When we went to the ranch for Easter, Mama was so afraid that we would contract tuberculosis that she tied red string on a place setting for silverware, which was to be used by no one but Paul. It was always sterilized by pouring scalding water from the teakettle over the pieces. None of the family was to use those utensils!

Paul stayed on the ranch for about six months until he had recuperated; then he went on his way. Mama was so relieved when Paul moved on.

☞ CELIA HILL'S JOURNAL ☜
CHAPTER FOURTEEN
Treasure to Trash— Trash to Treasure

One summer stands out in my memory quite clearly. I'm sure that it was during July or August, because our monsoon season didn't start until after July 4th. It had been raining on the north end of the ranch almost all afternoon. We had sat out on the front porch watching the lightning and listening to the thunder, thinking that surely the two creeks north of the ranch (Mexican Canyon and Fresno Canyon) would both run big.

About four o'clock in the afternoon, we heard a car coming up the canyon. We wondered who it could be, because only two kinds of people came along at that hour of the day: friends coming for a visit, or lost tourists who didn't have the slightest idea where they were or where they were going. Sure enough, there were three men from Houston in a big, fancy, two-seated car. The men were lost and looking for the road to Marfa. The car was similar to the ones in the ad. "It's Big! It's Beautiful! It's Buick."

Daddy told them that the road they were following would get them to Marfa, but he advised against it, pointing out that it was raining even at the moment. He suggested that they spend the night and get an early start the next morning. They were not to be deterred. Daddy told them that they shouldn't have any trouble finding the road because it followed the creek for approximately

CHAPTER FOURTEEN

sixteen miles until they climbed out of the canyon. They left with Daddy still trying to persuade them to stay the night.

Later that afternoon, we heard the roar of water and knew that the creek was on a big rise. We went out behind the ranch house to stand on the candelilla pile [chaff left over from a candelilla wax plant], where we had a good vantage point to watch the water run. The first water was so white that we knew it was from Fresno Canyon. Shortly, a wall of dark water came down, and we knew it was from Mexican Canyon. We hadn't been standing out there very long when we saw this huge object rolling over and over. As it swept by us in the current, we saw that it was the big fancy car from Houston.

Soon after daylight the next morning, the three bedraggled men came to the ranch exceedingly angry. They claimed it was Daddy's fault that they had literally driven up the creek bed following wagon tracks from where the workers had been hauling mesquite wood or sotol heads. On one particularly smooth stretch, they had accelerated to forty to fifty miles an hour and had become entangled in the net wire fence across the creek. The wall of water caught them there and swept them down the creek. They became separated, with two staying together and the third alone. They spent the night thinking that the other had drowned.

When they arrived at the ranch, Mother offered to cook them breakfast. I can remember how rude they were to her the whole time that they were eating. Except for the fact that Daddy wanted to get rid of them, he probably wouldn't have offered to take them to Marfa, where they could take a train back to Houston. Between them they made a deal that Daddy would take them to town, and in return he would get whatever he could salvage from the car that had become lodged against some huge rocks below the house. Due to water damage, there was not much salvageable. Daddy put the wheels from the car on the wagon. It made a lot easier riding! One man's trash is another man's treasure.

CELIA HILL'S JOURNAL
CHAPTER FIFTEEN
Rabbit Stew

Times were hard during the Depression. Mama was teaching school for $100 per month, and Daddy was raising goats for mohair and running a few cattle. We were out of groceries not only for the family, but for the goat herders as well.

Daddy, Winabeth, and Willeen went to Alpine, where Daddy talked to the banker asking if the bank would lend him some money until the price of mohair got better. Initially the banker said, "No, you have notes due now that you haven't made payment on, and we need to call those notes in."

In the meantime, Mama and I had stayed back on the ranch. All the goat herders had come in due to the lack of groceries. They were taking the goats out for short day trips to graze and coming back in the evening. We had no meat, so early of a morning and late in the evening, two of the men and I would take a .22 rifle to hunt for cottontail rabbits. If we killed three or four, Mama and I kept one and gave the others to the men. They were allowed one potato each, a few beans, plus veggies from the garden. Flour was so scarce that Mama made biscuits and sent the men their share—so afraid she was that they would waste the flour.

We had a heavy rain during that week, so we started working on the road in order that Daddy and the two girls could get back home. Mama and I rode horseback while the workers walked,

CHAPTER FIFTEEN

Angora Goats—Oak Creek in Big Bend National Park. *Courtesy of the family of Celia Hill.*

carrying picks, shovels, and crowbars. We had to work nearly six miles of road down the canyon. What an exciting moment it was when Daddy and the girls finally arrived with the pickup loaded down with supplies. Our faith was once more renewed.

☞ CELIA HILL'S JOURNAL ☜
CHAPTER SIXTEEN
Chicken on Sunday

Our chickens ranged freely up and down the creek behind the house, but they came in to eat and roost at night. We raised them primarily for eggs. When we heard a hen cackling, Mama would send us down along the banks of the creek to find the egg. We would occasionally have fried chicken on Sunday, which was a real treat. We would use a .22-caliber rifle to kill the chicken. That way we didn't disturb the whole flock by chasing them around. We had to shoot them in the head so that we didn't ruin any meat.

At least twice a month during the summer, Mama would fry up a chicken and pack it in a large Mrs. Tucker's lard bucket along with macaroni or potato salad, and we would be off over the mesa to Madera Falls [now named Madrid Falls by Texas Parks and Wildlife] for a day of swimming, relaxation, and arrowhead hunting. It was on one of these outings that I saw my first copperhead snake. Winabeth was taking a nap on a large flat rock in the shade of some cottonwood trees. I climbed up on the rock to talk to her and saw this snake that had just come up on the rock on the far side. I started talking to her, "Winabeth, wake up, but don't move." As soon as she was awake and fully coherent, I told her to move quickly away from the snake. The snake was almost as startled as she was and quickly crawled away.

CHAPTER SIXTEEN

On our way home later that afternoon, we swung by the old Madrid Ranch to check on the figs. Sure enough they were ready to pick. We arrived home tired but happy, knowing that soon we would be coming back and there would be another session of making fig preserves.

☞ CELIA HILL'S JOURNAL ☜
CHAPTER SEVENTEEN
The Price of Pitayas

For those of you not so familiar with the Big Bend of Texas, the pitaya or strawberry-cactus [*Echinocereus stramineus*] is one of the most colorful cacti in bloom. It produces a delightful, flavored fruit. The fuchsia-colored blooms appear in April, and the fruit matures in July. It was always a treat in the summer for us to go pitaya picking. One year in particular is etched in my memory.

Right after lunch, Daddy and we three girls decided to go pick pitayas. We saddled our horses, with Daddy choosing a "green-broke" bronc he felt needed the exercise and experience. We rode up the canyon from the house about a mile and a half. There, the steep trail toward Sauceda winds back and forth up onto the mesa beyond Rincon Mountain, which rises behind the ranch house to the north. I have always wondered why the largest and juiciest pitayas grow in the black volcanic soil that is prevalent in that area.

Daddy and Winabeth each had kitchen tongs to pick the fruit off the cactus. Willeen and I used small sticks to lift the fruit off the cactus and then to scrape off the clusters of thorns. It was getting rather late, the sun was low in the sky, and we had been picking for some time. We each had filled our Mrs. Tucker's Lard buckets and were ready to start down the steep trail leading home. Daddy saw one more huge pitaya that was "too good to

CHAPTER SEVENTEEN

leave behind." Instead of getting off his horse to pick the berry, he leaned over out of the saddle and tried to reach it from the horse's back. As he leaned over to the right, the boot on the left side slipped upward and his spur caught the horse's flank. Instant rodeo! The show was on! Being in an off-balanced position like he was, Daddy soon bucked off onto the sharp lava rocks. The rocks cut a gash into his head. Blood began flowing down his face onto his shirt. We finally managed to catch the horse and to hold him steady while we got Daddy back in the saddle. I can remember how scared I was when Daddy began asking, "Where's Mama?" We told him, "She's at home, Daddy." He questioned Winabeth, "Do you know how to get back to the house? Do you know the way home?" True to her usual capabilities, Winabeth *did* know the way back.

Mama had become anxious and was more than a little concerned when we came in after dark with Daddy showing up with blood running all down the front of his shirt. A couple of the workers took care of our horses while we got him in the house and in the bed. Daddy remained in a semi-comatose condition for a couple of days. It was too far to go to the doctor, so nature took over and healed him.

Note: See page 38 and more of the document cited here to learn more about pitayas and volcanic soil: https://www.nrcs.usda.gov/Internet/FSE_MANUSCRIPTS/texas/bigbendTX2011/Big%20Bend%20National%20Park.pdf.

☞ CELIA HILL'S JOURNAL ☜
CHAPTER EIGHTEEN
Who Needs a Doctor?

Accidents are bound to happen on the ranch, and we had to use discretion as to which injuries merited the trip to the doctor or which ones could be handled at home. The severity of the injury often determined whether or not the victim took a ride into town. For example, when Moises Lujan, the Mexican worker who had his leg broken when a bronc reared up and fell over on him, needed medical help, he was taken to the doctor in Terlingua, a distance of about thirty miles. But when Adele Fraier, the daughter of some friends, came down to see us from El Paso and had an accident, she wasn't taken to the doctor. That story goes like this.

While we were hiking, Adele broke off a lechugilla thorn in her ankle. These can be quite toxic, so we knew it had to be removed. Daddy sharpened his pocketknife and sterilized it with alcohol. While the rest of us sat on her to hold her still, he proceeded to "operate." Adele screamed, calling us "barbarians" and a few other choice names. After the thorn was extracted, Daddy put "Dr. Cox's Barbed Wire Liniment" on the wound. What was good enough for the animals was good enough for man. It healed in a few days. She never came back.

One summer while we were visiting our grandparents in Brookshire, Texas, Mama had some moles removed that had been bothering her. After we came back home the incisions

CHAPTER EIGHTEEN

did not heal. It was an unusually hot summer, and Mama wore "muumuu" style dresses that hung loose and allowed air to flow around the wounds. The incisions, however, continued to get larger until one day Daddy came up from the barn with a new bottle of "Dr. Cox's Barbed Wire Liniment." He doctored Mama's sores, and they healed in record time.

It was always an exciting time when the shearers came to clip the goats. This usually took place in the early spring while we were still in school, so we didn't get to witness many of these events after we moved to Alpine to attend school. The mohair was separated into different piles according to the quality of the hair and the age of the goats. Scaffolding was built in which a tow sack was hung. It held three hundred pounds of hair. Someone would have to get down in the bag and pack this hair down.

On one occasion, Daddy was the one packing the mohair into the bag. Either getting up onto the scaffolding or climbing back out, he lost his balance and fell approximately ten to twelve feet, resulting in a broken collarbone. The nearest doctor at the time was in Marfa, a distance of seventy-five miles. It was not a simple feat to drive a standard-shift pickup truck that far over rough mountain roads with only one arm. The "impossible" just takes a little longer.

I even had my share of accidents. One accident happened while I was whittling a piece of wood outside the kitchen door. The knife blade slipped and cut my left hand between the thumb and forefinger. I grabbed my hand and rushed inside. "Look, Mama, I struck oil!" My hand was gushing blood. I remember Mama turning around quickly. She grabbed the kitchen counter to steady herself, then grabbed for my hand. She held my pulse at the wrist while she led me out to the screened in porch. She helped me on to the bed and then sat and held my arm wrapped in towels keeping pressure on the pulse for a long time until it quit throbbing and the bleeding subsided. Again Dr. Cox's Liniment was used to heal the wound with little scarring. I paid for that dearly, because I could not ride my horse without use of my left hand for pulling the saddle. It was two to three weeks until the wound healed.

For everyday ailments, Mama and Daddy used castor oil (regularly), Black Draught (regularly), Baby Percy AD, 666 Cough Syrup, Aunt Lydia's, mercurochrome (Monkey Blood), and Sloan's Liniment. We always followed the castor oil and Black Draught with half an orange. It was almost twenty years before I could sit down and enjoy eating an orange without "tasting" the castor oil or Black Draught!

The year before I started school, we were riding our stick horses on the hill in front of the house. My "horse" was a little frisky and bucked me off into some lechugilla, causing a thorn to jam into my right hand at the base of my little finger. Daddy tried to get it all out and thought he had. After I started school, however, I began having trouble with my hand. The pressure on my hand from playing on the "monkey bars" irritated the imbedded thorn, and it became abscessed. It had worked its way up to the base of the middle finger. Mama took me to see Dr. Craddock. Without giving me anything, he just pierced the skin with a scalpel and abscess matter squirted over everything and everywhere. Dr. Craddock looked at Mama and said, "Mrs. Smith, I think you had better have a seat." Mama was rather large, and he knew if she fainted, he probably wouldn't be able to lift her by himself.

And finally, Enrique White, a son-in-law to the Carrascos who lived at the mouth of Fresno Creek, brought his son to the mine when it was located on the bank of the Fresno Creek. A rattlesnake had bitten the little boy, so they had put the boy's leg in a bucket with kerosene and had tied it at the knee. They came to the mine in a wagon pulled by mules, their only means of transportation. Daddy put the boy in his pickup truck and took him to Terlingua, where he received medical attention. I don't remember if they took him to the hospital in Alpine, but I do know that he made a full recovery.

Angora Goats (Harris with pipe). *Courtesy of the family of Celia Hill.*

Photo taken from Alpine, looking north. *Courtesy of David Keller.*

Fresno Mine. *Courtesy of the family of Celia Hill.*

View of Alpine. *Courtesy of the family of Celia Hill.*

Harris on a horse. *Courtesy of the family of Celia Hill.*

Fresno Mine. *Courtesy of the family of Celia Hill.*

View of Alpine. *Courtesy of the family of Celia Hill.*

Smith girls with a horse. *Courtesy of the family of Celia Hill.*

Floyd and friend with Winabeth and Bill Hill. *Courtesy of the family of Celia Hill.*

W. F. Donald, Celia Ann, Winabeth, Willeen, and Harris Smith. *Courtesy of the family of Celia Hill.*

Smith house in Fresno Canyon. *Courtesy of the family of Celia Hill.*

☞ CELIA HILL'S JOURNAL ☜
CHAPTER NINETEEN
Inspiration for Higher Education

Heretofore, we had always used one or two of the range cattle that were good milk producers for household milk. All three of us girls learned how to milk. Being the oldest, Winabeth was supposed to set the example for the other two of us. One evening when Daddy and the workers were later coming home, Mama and we girls went down to the corral to milk. At the time we had a black-and-white cow and a red brindle cow that we were milking. The black-and-white cow nearly always had to have hobbles even though she was probably the gentlest one. The brindle cow needed hobbles also, but she was more cantankerous. Winabeth was trying to milk her. The cow kicked off the hobbles and began slinging her head. She kicked the milk bucket (we always used a large Mrs. Tucker's lard bucket) out of Winabeth's hands, spilling what milk had been collected.

Winabeth became so enraged she threw the bucket at the cow. The bucket caught upside down on one of the cow's horns and the frightened cow began to run around in circles with the bucket clanging. Mama, Willeen, and I were laughing so hard we could not help at all. Needless to say, we didn't get much milk that night.

One day Daddy was looking at the black-and-white cow's teats and saw some small cut marks on them. These puzzled

CHAPTER NINETEEN

him. When he came to the house and asked us; of course no one knew. After examining our hands (fingernails) he discovered that Willeen's nails were unusually long. She had cut the cow as she was milking. He told her that she needed to cut her nails before she milked again. Fine with her; she just quit milking.

I can remember one day that Daddy came home so excited. It was about 1937 or 1938. He had bought a Jersey milch cow and a calf for about $50 (two for the price of one). It was the first real milch cow that we had ever had. To top it off, after only a month or so he discovered that the cow was pregnant. So, we actually got three for the price of one! The Jersey cows Pet, Shug, and Babe were excellent milk producers. The milk had the richest cream. I can remember having cream on peaches, figs, and pitayas during season.

For two years in a row the John Focht family from Austin came out to our ranch for their vacation. Dr. John Focht was the brother-in-law of Dr. Clifford B. Casey, who taught at Sul Ross State University for many years. There were three children in the Focht family: John, Tuck, and Faye Madeline. Faye Madeline and I were the same age. Tuck was about Willeen's age, and John a couple of years older. They had never experienced milking a cow, so we taught them that skill. Also, how to feed the cats at the same time.

During the drought season, Daddy would feed the milk cows the cabbage-like centers of the sotol plant as a supplement. It made the milk have a strong taste—not at all like the beverage "sotol" which is made from the same plant. When Daddy started mining and leased the ranch, I asked him if he would keep at least one of the Jersey cows so we could have fresh milk. "Only if you will be responsible for taking care of her and milking her twice a day," he told me.

"Not to worry." I saw it as no problem.

That was before I realized that nearly every day, no matter which direction I put her out to graze, she would double back and head up toward the ranch house. It was about two miles up Fresno Canyon to the first cross fence where she would be stopped. After so many days of hiking up there to find her and bringing her back down to the mine, I decided there must be an easier way. Early one morning, I thought how nice it would be to go to the market to buy a gallon of milk. There in was my inspiration for a higher education.

How many times since have I yearned for the "good old days" when we could skim fresh cream off the top of the milk pan and use some for fresh butter?

☞ CELIA HILL'S JOURNAL ☜
CHAPTER TWENTY
Decisions, Decisions

In 1938–1939, things were not going well in the ranching business. Mama and Daddy had to make decisions about the future. They decided that Mama would go back to school and complete the work for a degree while Daddy continued to hold on to the ranch. After she graduated and found a teaching job, then he would go back to school and complete the work for his bachelor's degree. The big decision now was: what to do with Willeen and Celia Ann?

In the fall of 1941, Willeen and I stayed with the Walter Measdays for about six weeks. Later, we stayed partly at home, but spent the nights with Edith and Cecil Hale, who lived behind us across the alley. We were sleeping on cots or the sofa; Edith was teaching school. This lasted about a month or less. Next, we stayed with the Charlie Chambers family for about two weeks. Marian Chambers was one of my best friends, so this arrangement suited the two of us just fine. They had their extra bedroom rented to the wife of an airman stationed at Marfa Army Air Field, so we slept on the sofa in the living room.

Then Mama and Daddy hired Miss Anne Morgan to come keep house for us and prepare meals. Two active high school girls proved to be more than she could manage, so that didn't last long.

First elementary school, Alpine—present day Sunshine House.
Courtesy of the family of Celia Hill.

☞ CELIA HILL'S JOURNAL ☜
CHAPTER TWENTY-ONE
From Rags to Riches

In 1939, everything changed, according to Celia's son, Rusty Hill, in a 2018 interview with Bill Wright.

After selling out his holding in the Chisos Mountains and moving to Fresno Canyon north of Lajitas, Daddy began expanding his ranching interests by buying railroad land at 35 cents more or less an acre, until he eventually owned forty sections of what is now the southern part of the Big Bend Ranch State Park. During the Depression and drought, Daddy realized he needed another source of income. Since his land was so near Terlingua and some of the geologic formations on the southern part of the ranch were similar to that around Terlingua, he encouraged the workers to look for signs of cinnabar ore and gave each of them a small sample. Some of the workers were from San Carlos, Mexico, and had worked in the mines.

It was in August that Martin Bernal, a one-armed goat herder, was the first one who found evidence of ore. He had his flock of goats watering at a *tinaja* in a cul-de-sac of small hills. A rainstorm came up, and as he walked back to camp to inspect for rain damage, he looked down and discovered that he was walking on cinnabar ore. Additionally, some of the goats that had lain down to rest were covered with red dirt on the underneath sides. When they got up to resume feeding, Martin

CHAPTER TWENTY-ONE

located a substantial specimen of ore and came to the ranch house early the next morning. Daddy realized the quality of the ore and left immediately to have the ore assayed in Marfa. The report came back favorable.

In an article by Winnie Smith in *Compressed Air Magazine* (March 1944), we learned that Harris had been an officer at the training camp at Leon Springs. He "exhibited a love for open country and pioneer life by establishing a ranch in the beautiful Chisos Mountains 90 mines south of Alpine. . . . He wanted to have a hand in the development of the last frontier of Texas, and took the first herd of registered Hereford cows into the river country for breeding purposes." After selling his holdings for a profit in 1929, he reinvested in the Fresno Canyon Ranch in Presidio County. For people who are familiar the area's great personalities, it will interest them to know that Harris purchased the Fresno ranch from J. E. Crawford—Hallie Stillwell's brother—in 1929. Like many people during the Great Depression, Harris carried a big debt and needed another source of income, so he decided to search for cinnabar on his own property. He gave his cowhands and goat herders some specimens of cinnabar and taught them how to take samples, promising a reward for any worthwhile find. The Mexican goat herder mentioned earlier proved to be the best prospector in the lot, and "in August of 1935, about two o'clock in the afternoon while watering his flock of Angora goats at a *tinaja* near his camp, a rainstorm came up suddenly and passed as quickly. Martin, soaked to the skin, headed for camp to see how it had withstood the storm and to change into dry clothes. When within a hundred yards of the place he glanced at the wet ground and at once realized that he was literally walking on cinnabar." Winnie adds, "Martin, in the course of time, received a satisfactory reward."

Daddy knew that he didn't have the expertise to develop a mine alone—or the finances—since he was already over his head in debt. (He once told me that he owed the Federal Land Bank in Dallas more money than anyone else in the state of Texas.) He did know that Homer Wilson, who had bought the Oak Creek Ranch in the Chisos Mountains, was also a mining engineer and geologist, having attended the Missouri School of Mines. Daddy contacted Mr. Wilson, who was in financial straits also, with the proposition of joining him in a business venture. A partnership was formed. They began to file claims and to prove up on these claims. Also, they acquired more land, which Homer thought appeared promising as a possible site for cinnabar ore.

Patricia Wilson Clothier tells in her memoir Beneath the Window: Early Ranch Life in the Big Bend before It Was a National Park *(Houston: Iron Mountain Press, 2003, 91, 92, and 169), that "Cinnabar, heavier than surrounding dirt, sank to the bottom when mixed with water. This made it easier to separate the quicksilver-bearing ore. Since these times during the Depression made starting a new mine difficult, they tried to keep expenses low." She also said about the partnership between her father and Celia's: "When a Mexican laborer found the first signs of a workable cinnabar, Harris Smith came to Daddy and said, 'You be the brains, Homer, and I'll be the brawn.'"*

With the advent of WWII and the increased demand for mercury, the Fresno Mines launched into operation on June 1, 1939. Starting out on the bank of Fresno Creek with a small flotation process and retorts to treat the concentrates, this process soon proved to be inadequate and overly expensive. In order to raise enough funds to convert to a six-ton furnace which would produce a flask of mercury a day, Daddy sold his last flock of Angora goats—the "cream of the crop" of his registered goats—in 1941. The mining operation was moved closer to the source of ore. The ore proved to be so rich and abundant that the operation changed over to a thirty-ton Cottrell furnace that yielded a flask of mercury per ton of ore.

The success of the mining operation was such that both Homer Wilson and Daddy were able to pay off their debts on

CHAPTER TWENTY-ONE

their ranch holdings. Martin received compensation as long as the mine produced mercury.

In its heyday, Fresno Mines resulted in a small community being established by the name of Buena Suerte. There were twelve small one-room cabins with water and electricity furnished to Anglo workers, while the Hispanic workers were furnished three- to four-room rock apartments with a central water supply. There was a schoolhouse and a general store, both made of native stone. A post office was established in the spring of 1943, [when the town had] a population of more than two hundred people.

The store was quite large because it held provisions for two hundred people—everything from over-the-counter medications to needles and thread. Fresh produce and meats were brought in on the mail truck. In the back of the store was an ice room that had very thick walls and heavily insulated doors. Two-hundred pound blocks of ice were brought down from Alpine that helped keep products cold and prevented spoilage. A great assortment of canned goods was available.

There was a variety of clothing on hand. We were greatly amused when one of the older workers came in and bought a pair of underwear to fit Mama. He wanted Daddy to wait on him because he was embarrassed to ask one of the girls. It turned out that he wanted to buy a pair of underwear for his wife. Daddy asked him what size; the man looked around a minute and studied the problem, finally he told Daddy that he needed a pair that would fit Mrs. Smith.

Attached to the store were additional rooms that were used by the bookkeepers. In one of them was a telephone that connected with the shop and another one at the furnace. This was one of the old phones that had a handle on it. The rings were one short and one long, or two long and one short, etc. for the different locations.

Books of coupons in different denominations from $5 to $25

could be purchased. Each book had coupons from $.01 to $5 that could be redeemed at the company store.

During the war, Fresno Mines produced one-tenth of all the mercury that was produced in the United States. Dr. Lockhart, from Alpine, was stationed in the Philippines. As they operated in their field hospitals, he would count the bombs falling around them. He would count to ten and tell one of his nurses, Evelyn Burnham Fulcher, that that bomb was from Harris Smith. It was from Evelyn's father that Daddy had bought the Oak Creek ranch.

With the end of the war and a decrease in the demand for mercury, Fresno Mines was shut down late in 1944 or early 1945. The site of Buena Suerte is now among the tours of the ghost towns in the Lajitas area.

"The ore was so pure that you could hold a cigarette lighter underneath a 25-pound rock and mercury would come out. It's that freaking pure," Rusty noted adding that that his grandfather *"was crankin' out a good 30–40 percent of the mercury that was ever produced from South County."*

In Jim Glendenning's interview for Marfa Public Radio, Celia answers Jim's question about how well the mine did with "Very well. During the war years that little mine produced 10 percent of the mercury in the whole United States." She adds, "We had about two hundred families living in the community. We had enough that a Post Office was established in 1943. And the community [was called] Buena Suerte. And my mother was the postmistress and my aunt, Mrs. Bledsoe, was the schoolteacher."

The following is from the Jim Glendenning interview of Celia Hill for Marfa Public Radio Voices of the Big Bend Program, Ruidosa, Texas, at the store and home of Celia Hill, October 2007.

The mining years coincided with Celia's teen years. She told Jim about an adventure with some girlfriends who decided to take their horses home for the summer from Alpine to Terlingua—a 122-mile trip.

Fresno Mine. *Courtesy of the family of Celia Hill.*

In addition to attending movies with Roy Rodgers, Dale Evans, and Tom Nix for fifteen to twenty cents a head, Celia and her girlfriends "who liked to ride horses ... worked on many of the ranches all the way from Ryan, which is between Marfa and Valentine, over to some of the ranches around Fort Davis, back over to the Merriweather Ranch, just north of Alpine. We rounded up sheep. We rounded up cattle. We helped brand. We just did everything the men would have done except the roping. We didn't do a lot of roping. We had a wonderful time."

Robbie reflected on this period of prosperity, saying that her family didn't really change lifestyles. They remained frugal and did not take any fancy trips. But at age sixteen, their mother, Winnie Donald Smith, became ill, had surgery, and died on December 23, 1944. Celia graduated from Alpine High School the next spring. Surely Celia's horse, "Pinochle," and rides with her friend Maxine were a great help in these days.

Fresno Mine. *Courtesy of the family of Celia Hill.*

Fresno Mine. *Courtesy of the family of Celia Hill.*

Fresno Mine. *Courtesy of the family of Celia Hill.*

☞ CELIA HILL'S JOURNAL ☜
CHAPTER TWENTY-TWO
Dummy

Norberto Rios was the son of Manuel Rios, our neighbor. He was born a deaf-mute; the Anglo men referred to him as "Dummy." Consequently, he was the perfect choice to work the rock crusher at the mine. Since the rock crusher was at the highest point of elevation of the processing plant, "Dummy" had a spectacular view of the surrounding area. He could see approximately five miles down the road and could tell by the cloud of dust that a car was coming.

When "Dummy" detected a car, he commenced making an undue amount of noise, alerting everyone in the area. If it happened to be Border Patrol, they would arrive on the scene to find a skeleton crew working because all of the illegals would be over the hill in the next arroyo or behind mesquite bushes, out of sight. If it were anyone else, it wouldn't make a difference.

Not only was "Dummy" a good worker on the rock crusher, but also he was one of the best horsemen I ever knew. He could ride and rope like few other Mexicans, and he could train a horse to perfection.

☞ CELIA HILL'S JOURNAL ☜
CHAPTER TWENTY-THREE
Mail Truck Swamper

I remember one such trip quite well when it had rained all over Brewster County. We left Alpine around noon on Friday, and we had to wait for several creeks to run down. Calamity Creek and Butcher Knife were the largest. It was still raining when we got to Kennedy Flats, which was one big, sticky, clay mud bog. We averaged one mile per hour crossing those flats. It isn't easy getting a large trailer truck fully loaded with freight unstuck from the mud. We finally made it in to Terlingua at 2:30 a.m. Willeen and I slept on pallets at the Brown's house until daylight when we went down to unload freight for Terlingua. It was noon or past by the time we arrived at the Fresno Mines. I felt like I had more than earned my passage that trip.

During the war years, rubber was a precious commodity. I can remember one time that Ernest Acton was having trouble getting spare tires for his truck. He asked Daddy to help secure these tires. Daddy wrote to the congressman and the Administration of the War Ration Board explaining the need for tires. The congressman wrote back from behind his desk in Washington, DC, and directed that the supplies be shipped by rail. Daddy was furious. He responded with the suggestion that the congressman take a closer look at the map of the area, get better acquainted with his constituents and their circumstances. Furthermore, if they expected to continue receiving mercury for the war effort, he needed to see that tires were made available for freight trucks. He did! They were!

Street scene—Alpine, Texas. *Courtesy of the family of Celia Hill.*

Brewster County Courthouse—Alpine, Texas. *Courtesy of the family of Celia Hill.*

Alpine High School. *Courtesy of the family of Celia Hill.*

☞ CELIA HILL'S JOURNAL ☜
CHAPTER TWENTY-FOUR
Beating the Rubber Shortage

While attending school in Alpine, I sorely missed the ranch and riding my horse. With a great deal of persuasion, I managed to talk Mama and Daddy into letting me bring two of the horses (mine and Willeen's) to Alpine. Dr. Clifford Casey was generous enough to let us keep them at his riding stables that he had near the college. Our horses were both pacers; consequently, they proved to be extremely popular with the female students. They were so popular that many times they were ridden two and three times a day on the weekend without much rest. As a result, they both lost weight. I worried about them so much that I fixed the fence around our backyard and brought them down to the house. It was a lot of work keeping that lot cleaned.

When school was out for the summer of 1943, we were faced with the problem of getting the horses back to the ranch, 120 miles away. Two of my friends and I, with no little amount of trouble, talked our parents into letting us ride the horses down south. June Joyce Atkinson was to ride Willeen's horse, Generosa. Marian Chambers Bridge had her own horse, Chappo, which she would ride, and I was to ride my own horse, Calcitin.

We must have made plans for almost a month before the event took place. Finally, the date was set, and we were to leave Alpine June 3rd. Things were not all in our favor, as the horses

CHAPTER TWENTY-FOUR

got out of the backyard during the night. It was about 9:00 a.m. by the time we rounded them up and got on our way. We rode approximately twenty miles before we stopped for lunch. Mama and Willeen met us with a picnic lunch, which we ate under a cedar tree on the side of the road.

Later in the afternoon, Charlie Chambers, Marian's dad, came along to make camp and spend the night with us since there were only seven ranch houses visible from the road. I asked him, "How far down the road are you going before you make camp?" His reply was, "Just keep riding until you see me on the side of the road."

After going through the land along the west side of the Elephant Mountains, we started through Green Valley. The road stretched out ahead of us for miles. Black Mesa and Santiago Peak loomed high to east. We rode and rode. It got hotter and hotter. We could see Nine Point Mesa ahead of us to the southeast. Beyond that were the Corazones. To the southwest were Agua Fria Mountain and Packsaddle Mountain. The Solitario Range was on the horizon to the west. Our destination lay at the far southern edge of those mountains. Too bad we couldn't just cut across country, but there were too many impenetrable canyons and miles of mal pais [bad country], which was impossible unless you were quite familiar with the few trails that traversed the area. Too, there was no guarantee that the tinajas would have water in them, so we stuck to the road.

The sun started going down. It began to get dark, and still there was no sign of a campfire. Finally, thirty-two miles down the road from our lunch break (a total of fifty-two miles in one day) we saw the welcome glow of the campfire. It was 9:00 p.m. Charlie had set up camp in a corner of the fence line near a windmill where we could water the horses. They could graze a little and at least lie down to rest as we so willingly did.

Before setting out on our journey early the next morning, Charlie took pictures of us (on horseback), one of which was published in the *Fort Worth Star-Telegram* with the caption "Beating the Rubber Shortage."

We continued on our way to Terlingua. It was a hot day. We ran out of water somewhere around Kennedy Flats. And there was a lack of shade anywhere. We ate sandwiches on the go. Terlingua Creek was a welcome sight when we finally reached it near 6:00 p.m. To our dismay, when we arrived in Terlingua we found that we were too late for dinner at the hotel where meals were served boarding-house style.

Being accustomed to making the most of the situation, we went to the local ice cream parlor. There we were greeted by a couple of squads of soldiers who had been sent to guard the mercury mines at Terlingua. They couldn't believe that we three teenage girls had ridden from Alpine, a distance of one hundred miles, in two days. Needless to say, we didn't spend one dime, but had all the ice cream we could eat.

When we went to our room at the motel, we discovered that we had two twin beds for the three of us. We tried sleeping crossways in the beds, which kept rolling. We didn't get much sleep that night.

On the third day we rode the final twenty-two miles to Buena Suerte, reaching our destination about 2:00 p.m.—the end of a long ride to our summer home.

☞ CELIA HILL'S JOURNAL ☜
CHAPTER TWENTY-FIVE
Pulling Up Slack

Upon entry of the United States into WWII in 1941, there was a shortage of men to work on the ranches of the Tri-County area. Consequently, several of us girls who were best friends and who owned horses, were recruited to work on the ranches during spring and fall round up. (This group included Marian Chambers, June Joyce Atkinson, and Helen and Maxine Acton.)

I asked Daddy to bring my horse to town. He also brought Willeen's horse, even though she didn't take part in the ranch work. June Joyce Atkinson usually rode Willeen's horse; Marian Chambers had her own horse. We worked on the Mulhern, the Tippitt, the Merriwether, and the Ryan Ranches. We worked for Maynard "Dutch" Acton, who was foreman for Worth Evans.

Dutch was the father of Maxine—later Cox, and Helen—later Bell. The five of us would round up in the fall for shipping and in the spring for marking and branding. When the cattle work would be finished, we worked sheep to be shipped or sheared. Many a weekend I would leave Alpine early enough Saturday morning to reach the Merriwether, a distance of seven miles, in time to help Tony drive in the remuda for the day's work.

Maxine told us that they worked as cowgirls on this ranch that her father managed. Leased to Worth Evans by the Merriwether family,

CHAPTER TWENTY-FIVE

the girls' labors included flanking the animals—laying them out with one girl at the head and another stretching out a leg—for ear clipping, vaccinating, and branding.

On the weekends that we drove to Ryan, Dutch would make a loop through Alpine to pick us girls up by five to six p.m. I can vouch for how cold it would be in the back of the pickup on an early March day. We would be out on the slopes of Haystack Mountain some mornings while the frost still covered the rockslides and the wild roses. Maxine's cousin, Brooks Acton, and Bub Evans, son of Worth Evans, both lived in Fort Davis. They were in high school as were we girls. Sometimes they would bring friends and come over to help in the works [working the cattle].

Maxine chuckled during her interview recalling the fun her parents were. Another example of this follows in the last chapter of Celia's journal.

On Saturday night Dutch and his wife, also named Celia, would take us in to Alpine to the last movie. She would use her milk and egg money earned by selling fresh produce in Alpine during the week.

Mrs. J. D. Harris was the movie ticket seller during those days. When she saw our group coming, she would throw up her hands and exclaim, "Wait a minute, I have to get my pen and paper out for this bunch!" After we got back to the ranch, we would stay up until 1:30 or 2:00 a.m. playing "Flinch." Dutch would call out, "You kids better go to bed now 'cause you're going to have to roll out at 5:00 a.m." Several times in early spring one group would pike [dare] the other to jump in the tank for an early morning swim.

Those were the days when all the ranches were on a party telephone line and were using crank phones. We listened to whether it rang one short, two long, or any number of combinations to know who was on the line. John Dow Harris worked for the telephone company after school and on weekends. He always knew when we were at the Merriwether and would break in on our phone conversations if he were working out in that area.

One morning after riding out from Alpine, I was standing by the cook camp trying to warm up. Old Jess asked, "Missy, don't you want a cup of coffee?"

"No, Jess, I don't drink coffee," I replied.

"Missy, this mawning you needs a cup of coffee!" And he poured one up for me. I'll admit it tasted good. I used it as much to warm my hands as to warm my stomach.

It was during this time that I realized what true racism was. One morning Little Jess, Old Jess's son, came in to eat in the kitchen. I sat down at the table just to talk to him. I don't remember the gist of the conversation. I think it touched on why he hadn't been drafted, but it came out that he was illiterate. I was appalled—this was the 1940s! Everyone should be able to read and write, even Little Jess!

His father, Old Jess, was a direct descendant of the Buffalo Soldiers who had been stationed in Fort Davis. He married a Mexican woman. There was no school for Negroes in Fort Davis. Little Jess wasn't a Mexican, so he couldn't attend the school for children of Mexican descent. He had been denied an education of any kind. What an injustice!

He was the handsomest black man I had ever seen and was undoubtedly one of the best cowboys that I had ever observed.

☞ CELIA HILL'S JOURNAL ☜
CHAPTER TWENTY-SIX
Don't Fence Me In

One Saturday, Marian and I were tired of riding up and down the streets or out along the highways, so we headed out to Sunny Glen. We hadn't ridden very far up into the canyon when we saw an open gate and decided to go through it. This led about one and a half miles into a box canyon.

Upon our return a short time later, we discovered that the gate was not only closed, but it was locked. Marian said, "Celia Ann, what are we going to do?" I knew for a fact that we weren't going to sit there waiting for whomever to come back.

"I have an idea. I know where we are, we'll go over the mesa and come down on the other side at Dutch and Celia Acton's." We rode back up into the canyon. After a careful search, we found a deer trail leading up out of the canyon. Since both of our horses were well-shod and good mountain ponies, it didn't take us too long to climb out on top to face another problem. We ran into another fence across our path.

This time we used rocks to knock the staples out of the posts for two lengths. One of us stood on the wire, holding it down while the other very carefully led the horses over so they didn't get caught in the wire. Then we hammered the staples back in the posts after we had straightened the wire back up.

We circled back far enough up the mesa so that we didn't have to cross any more canyons. I had been up in the area several times

CHAPTER TWENTY-SIX

gathering cattle or sheep, so I knew where I was. We finally made it down into the canyon where the Merriwether Ranch is by 3:00 p.m. The Actons were so surprised to see us. I had a hard time explaining to Dutch just how we made it across the mountains. He was shaking his head as he went out to have Tony, one of the workers, turn our horses loose.

They thought it was too late for us to ride the seven miles back to Alpine, so we called our folks and told them where we were. We delighted in using the old crank telephone that they had. I never did find out whose land we were on. I did always wonder what he thought of the horse tracks going in, but never coming back out.

Celia and Winabeth. *Courtesy of the family of Celia Hill.*

CELIA HILL'S JOURNAL
CHAPTER TWENTY-SEVEN
Our Senior Trip

Since we were still experiencing the effects of gasoline rationing, rubber shortage, and a few more minor inconveniences as a result of the war, we were very limited on the extent of our school activities. Not to be daunted by these, a few of us decided that we should go on a senior trip. I contacted Ernest Acton, who had been our mailman to the mine and still carried supplies to Terlingua. I asked him what it would take to haul our senior class of twenty-seven and the necessary sponsors down to the mine and thence to the ranch house. He agreed to do this for $1.00 per head.

We set to making plans: planning for the meals for Friday, Saturday, and part of Sunday, and collecting the necessary money from each one anticipating on going on the trip. I think we spent less than $10.00 per person.

On Friday morning, we were all ready to go with Mrs. Johnnie Joyce and Mrs. Celia Acton accompanying us on the trip. We left school around 9:00 a.m. with the students and their bedrolls all in the back of the truck. We sang songs, played games, and slept. About halfway, we stopped for lunch, and then went on to the mine where we met my father and my aunt.

There we divided the boys and girls into groups and chose our cabins for the night. Some went hiking while others helped set up camp and prepare the evening meal. Wood had to be

CHAPTER TWENTY-SEVEN

gathered and a circle built for our campfire. After supper, we told stories, sang songs, and pointed out constellations in the sky. June Joyce had bought her accordion, which was always fun.

Early Saturday morning we loaded up the truck and went up to the ranch house where all those desiring to do so went swimming. We had lunch, then went back to the mine. Sunday morning came all too early. Begrudgingly, we loaded up for our return trip to Alpine. Since the weather begins to get hot around the middle of May, by the time we got back to Alpine, we were all sunburned, completely exhausted, and contented.

Maxine Acton Cox shared a bit of humor about this day—May 10, 1945. She said that her father woke them up the next morning with a record playing on the Victrola: "Get Ready, Hesy!" Jess fixed breakfast and then they went to work.

The night we graduated, May 25, 1945, our teachers allowed us to stay up late and party in the home economics lab until 2:30–3:00 a.m. Soon we all went down to see several of our classmates leave for the Service, not knowing when, or if, we would see them ever again.

That night the word "commencement" took on a special meaning for all of us.

Celia Smith at Sul Ross State. *Courtesy of the family of Celia Hill.*

☞ CELIA HILL'S JOURNAL ☜
CHAPTER TWENTY-EIGHT
My Last Cattle Drive

After the mine was shut down in 1944, Daddy decided to go back into ranching. This time around he wanted to try the corriente cattle from Mexico. They would climb higher on the mountains and forage and would travel much farther to and from water than the registered Herefords.

Daddy met a friend of his from Mexico in Lajitas and arranged for his friend to get approximately four hundred head of cattle from the neighboring ranches and bring them to Ojinaga, fifty miles more or less upriver from Lajitas. On the appointed date, which was in July 1945, we met the Mexican rancher in Ojinaga. One of our workers had brought a remuda, which was composed of only a few horses—ten to twelve at most—through the Boficillas Mountains over to Presidio. We got permission to ride our horses across the river to receive the cattle. We rode out on the hills near the stock pens of Ojinaga. The hills were littered with carcasses of cattle that were victims of either drought or hoof and mouth disease.

While we were waiting around, one of the cattle buyers from El Paso, Jess Burner, approached me as I sat on my horse in the shade of a cottonwood tree. "You interested in selling that horse, young lady?" Mr. Burner inquired.

"If the price is right," I replied.

CHAPTER TWENTY-EIGHT

"I've been looking for a horse that my girls could ride. How much do you want for him?" he asked.

"I'll take $100.00 for him as is," I answered.

"Bring him by the stock pens in Presidio and leave him in one of the pens. Come by the motel and I'll have a check waiting for you," Mr. Burner directed.

When Daddy came back to where I was waiting for him, I said, "Daddy, I sold my horse."

"How much did you get for him?" he asked.

"I got $100.00." And I told him about the arrangements Mr. Burner and I had made.

Daddy rode over and talked to Mr. Burner to verify that the trade was made; it was my horse. When he came back, he told me, "That horse wasn't worth more than $75.00 on the best horse market. Now you have only one horse to ride all the way back home." It was one of the hardest things I ever did to leave my horse in the stockyards and walk away while he was pacing back and forth along the fence nickering to me.

When we went by the motel to pick up the check, Daddy had to go in to get it. I looked at the check through teary eyes; it was hard to believe that my horse had been reduced to a piece of paper.

I always wondered how long it took them to find out that the horse kicked like the devil. We always had to tie up one leg and sometimes throw him to put shoes on his back feet. "How long did they keep that horse?" I wondered.

We drove the cattle across the old wooden bridge, for a price of twenty-five cents per head, through downtown Presidio to the stockyards on the east side of town. Early the next morning we took them out to Fort Leaton (Fortin), which belonged to Mr. Skaggs at the time. Daddy leased a field just below the fort for a week to give the cattle a chance to gain some weight and rest up in preparation for the long drive back down the river to Fresno Canyon through the Boficillos via Sauceda.

My Last Cattle Drive

We camped out in Fort Leaton for a week. My aunt Elizabeth Bledsoe and I were camp cooks. We were up early riding the fences around the field every day to be sure that none of the cattle had gotten out. The first day we hit the trail for home, we herded the cattle down the highway to Ternero Draw and then up the arroyo to Chupadero for the first night. We spent the second night on the trail before we reached Sauceda.

The cattle had been without water for two days by the time we reached Sauceda. Since the water trough was on a float system, I was designated to sit at the end of the trough and hold the float down to keep the water flowing steadily into the trough. It was while I was so engaged that a spotted face, cross-eyed cow came up for water. I had never seen a cross-eyed before and almost fell off the trough from laughing so hard. Besides being startled at my laughter, I think the poor critter was seeing me double and was hesitant to stay and drink her fill.

We were up and on our way to Fresno Canyon early the fourth day. We reached the creek early enough to get the cattle watered and settled down before we went on home. In the whole drive we lost only three young calves. Every day my uncle Lige (Elijah) Bledsoe would shuttle the weakest calves by picking [them out] all the way to Casa Piedra and the thirty-five miles down Fresno Canyon to the headquarters where they were put on milk cows.

About ten days later, I left for my first year of college at Texas Tech.

Celia's son Rusty told Bill Wright that he'd "match my mom's horse sense against any man I've met in my life."

Celia considered her decision to go to Texas Tech a mistake because it was too big. She told Jim Glendenning that she felt both frightened and out of context. There she ended up getting into a marriage that failed before going home to Sul Ross, where she knew all the professors. Her first bachelor's degree was in accounting and agriculture.

CHAPTER TWENTY-EIGHT

Texas Tech Yearbook, *La Ventana*, 1946. Celia Smith is the last person on the right. *Courtesy of* La Ventana *Yearbook, Texas Tech University.*

Celia's friend Maxine Acton Cox said that she headed to Sul Ross for two years after high school, as Celia headed off to Texas Tech. Maxine never met Celia's first husband Cotton Sims, but she reconnected with Celia after Celia married Robert Hugh Hill. Maxine married an Ohioan named Buck in 1947. They lived and worked on a ranch in Valentine. The couples got together for barbeques and exchanged letters and cards. Maxine recalled that Celia and Bob kept a de-scented skunk for a pet during this time. The Coxes attended Robert's funeral in 1981.

The Sacred Heart of the Church of Jesus in Ruidosa, TX. *Courtesy of Bill Wright.*

Portrait of Celia Hill by Bill Wright. *Courtesy of Bill Wright.*

Celia with visitors from Oman—La Junta General Store. *Courtesy of Bill Wright.*

☞ CELIA HILL'S JOURNAL ☜
CHAPTER TWENTY-NINE
Return to a Remote Canyon Paradise

I n 2008, Celia had gone to see her daughter, Roxie, in San Antonio and came back feeling tired. Having survived breast cancer and a mastectomy at age fifty-five, she couldn't get her energy back. But she was still walking a mile every day of the week before a sudden illness came on when she was eighty.

Then she quit walking, and with bad diarrhea, she went to a doctor in Presidio. The doctor told Rusty to take her home and if she didn't get better, call 911. Rusty called Robbie the night after this doctor visit and said that their mom was lethargic and had not eaten or gotten up since she'd been to the doctor.

Celia did not get up the next day, so an ambulance was called, and she was put on a breathing machine in Alpine. Robbie's doctor sent her mom to Odessa, where the medication they gave her made her delirious. She was put on a ventilator overnight. The next day she said goodbye, and soon she was gone. The doctor said that the pneumonia had taken her life but suspected the cancer had come back—this time into her spine.

A memory stone was placed in the Alpine cemetery in her honor. Then her ashes were taken back to the place where she grew up and spread on top of the mountain, so that she had a view of the mine and area she'd roamed in her early years. She was home in her remote canyon paradise.

CELIA SMITH HILL FAMILY TREE

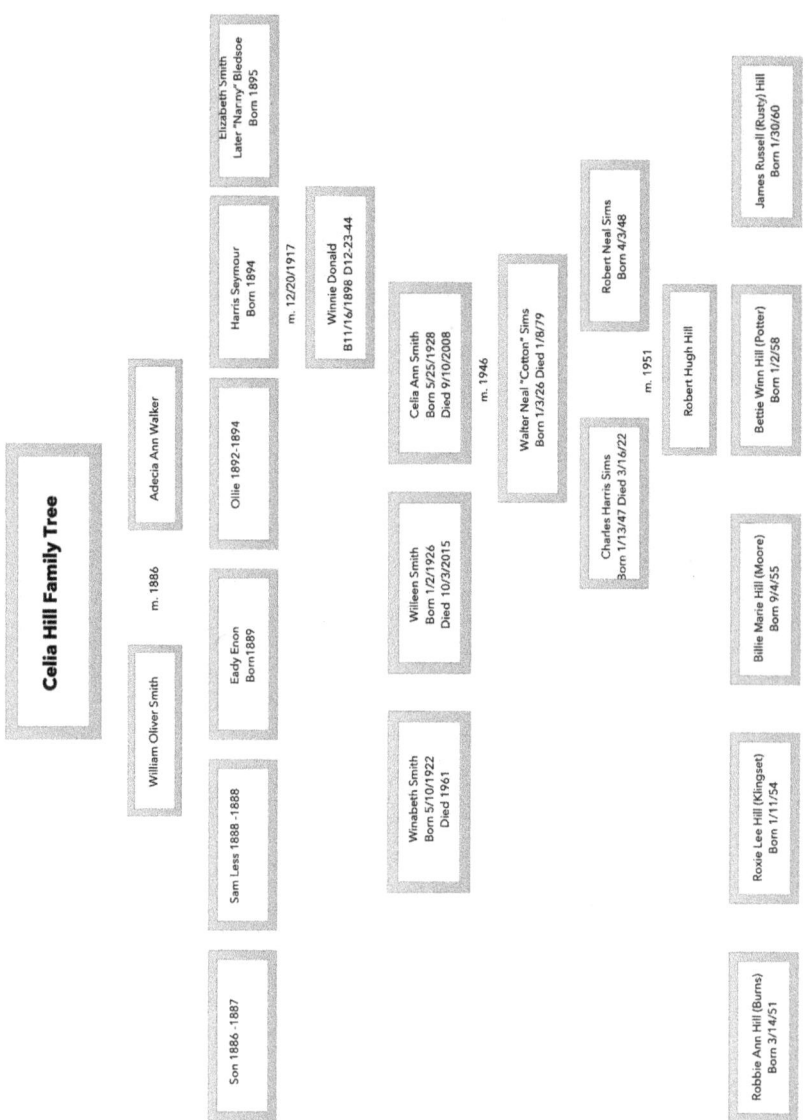

Celia Smith Hill Family Tree. *Courtesy of Marianne Wood.*

CELIA HILL TIMELINE

1886	William Oliver Smith and Adecia Ann Walker marry in Memphis, TN.
1908	Celia's father comes to Alpine with his parents. He builds the first frame house in Alpine, on the creek.
1928	Celia Ann Hill is born on May 25.
1929	The Smith family moves into Fresno Canyon.
1939	Cinnabar ore is discovered in Fresno Canyon, eleven miles north of Lajitas.
1944	The mine is shut down, and Celia's dad decides to get back into the ranching business.
1945	(July) Celia goes to Mexico to help her dad drive back some cattle and sells her horse for $100.
1945	Celia graduates from Alpine High School and leaves for Texas Tech.
1946	Celia marries Walter Neal "Cotton" Sims. Two children, Cotton Sims and Robert Neal, are born in Tulia, Texas, in 1947 and 1948.
1947	About this time, Celia returns to Alpine.
1951	Celia marries Robert Hugh Hill.
1951	Celia graduates from Sul Ross. Robbie Hill is born on March 14 in Alpine.
1951	Celia begins teaching school in Leakey, Texas.

CELIA HILL TIMELINE

1953 Celia moves to Banquete in South Texas. She keeps books for the Robstown School District.
1955 Billie is born in Kingsville.
1958 Bettie is born in Kingsville.
1960 Rusty is born in Robstown.
1961 Celia moves to Imperial Texas and teaches school there.
1963 Celia moves to Glenwood, New Mexico, and teaches with her husband in a two-room schoolhouse.
1965 Celia teaches in Roswell, New Mexico.
1968 Celia takes the children to Geneseo, New York, and points in between.
1969 Celia and Robert Hill divorce.
1979 Walter Neal "Cotton" Sims dies in Tulia, Texas.
1979 Robert Hugh Hill retires from teaching in California and moves to Alpine.
1981 Celia teaches school in Pecos.
1981 Robert Hugh Hill dies of peritonitis of the liver in November.
1982 Celia works in the Alpine liquor store while she and Rusty live in a gaudy pink house.
1983 Celia moves to Terlingua, Texas, where she teaches school.
1987 Celia leaves Terlingua with a man named Herb

CELIA HILL TIMELINE

Haas—a cousin. (They had Grandmother Eady Enon Smith Haas in common.) Celia and Herb separate after about five years, and she moves to Presidio and teaches English.

1989 Celia moves to Las Cruces, New Mexico, and teaches in Anthony.

1991 Celia moves to Presidio and teaches school. While she is there, she meets her last husband, John Littlejohn. He takes people on mule trips to Mexico and serves as a hunting guide in Colorado.

1996 John finds the store in Ruidosa and talks Celia into buying it. They run the store together for about three years before John's death.

1998 Celia retires from teaching after thirty-nine-and-a-half years.

John Littlejohn dies. Robbie described this marriage as happy.

1999 Celia's La Junta General Store sells mainly beer and ice cream. But because so many people drive up to Hot Springs not realizing there was not any food available, Celia adds some Spam and Vienna Sausages and crackers.

2008 Celia dies on September 10 following a short illness.

MAP OF PRESIDIO COUNTY

Presidio County Map. *Courtesy of the* Texas Almanac.

APPENDIX
"Show 990" Transcript: Bob Phillips interview with Celia Hill[2]

BP (Bob Phillips): They rise and fall hiding the dusty remnants of ancient secrets. It's a place where the wind is the only voice of the rugged peaks stretch to the sky. The Chihuahuan Desert of West Texas is a barren, empty, silent place, and in what's left of a tiny village called Ruidosa, Celia Hill operates the only store for miles and miles around.

CH (Celia Hill): You don't see something like this in the city. You'd be surprised at how many days we've gone without anybody coming in the store—nobody.

BP: Perched on the bank of the Rio Grande, Celia's La Junta General Store has to be the most remote shopping establishment anywhere.

CH: Well I'm particularly amused at the people that the people who come down here and the young people more than anything else but a few of the older ones: "How far is it to the nearest mall?"

BP: (laughs)

---
2 *Courtesy of the* Texas Country Reporter.

APPENDIX

CH: O-kay! And how far is it to Walmart? Well, But, if we want our nearest Walmart is in Chihuahua City 165 miles away (BP: in another country). CH: In another country. But if we want to go to Walmart here we have to go all the way to Odessa or El Paso. I don't spend my time being lonely. I don't think about it. (Mighty! Come on!)

BP: Now usually it's a misguided tourist or a lost driver who are her customers.

CH: If they haven't been forewarned or just forgot to bring food with them we try to keep a few snacks here so that they can keep their stomach off their backbone (chuckling) so to speak. We have tuna, which I think is real good in the foil packages. We have juice—quite an assortment of juice for people to drink. We have these little snack packs—of course Spam and Vienna sausages they're always—Beanee Weenees—they're always a good something to have around. Anytime you have Beanee Weenees or peanut butter—why, what more could you want?

BP: Now groceries only cover one shelf of Celia's little store. The rest she calls her Little Museum.

CH: I've wanted to show you something that I have in here.

BP: Mementos of a life spent deep in a remote desert canyon.

CH: This is the last blanket that we have that was made from the hair of the mohair—of the goats that we had on our ranch. And every year when they would shear the goats, Daddy would send one sack of hair over to Mexico, and they made blankets or saddle blankets—whatever out of that, and this is one of the last ones that we have so I'm kinda proud of it.

BP: Her life and her history belong to a rocky valley called Fresno Canyon Ranch. Celia's entire childhood was spent barefoot in the desert away from towns, away from people. The old home place now in ruins was swallowed by Big Bend Ranch State Park. A few years ago Celia decided to put her memories to paper, and now with her assistant Mariposa copying it all down in pencil and ballpoint pen, Celia slowly recites the memories of a lifestyle that can never be recaptured.

CH: There aren't too many people still living that have the kind of history that I do. It is about the years we lived in this remote canyon that these stories are told. And then I go on from there.

I've told about the hard times and the good times. We had some difficult times because this was 1929, which was during the Depression. Here I was living 122 miles from a community—a town of any size. And I had to walk and get that cow every afternoon because she kept trying to go back up to the ranch and I decided right then I would go to school and I would earn enough money that I could buy milk. And sure enough there times now that I wish I had those big pans of nice milk with nice rich cream on them because we had some good jersey cows.

BP: Day in and day out under the front porch shade Celia sifts through the stories uninterrupted by crowds or distractions.

CH: Oh, this is the way I like it. Yes. When somebody comes in, I take time and visit with them and enjoy them, but when you're gone I'm not going to sit here and worry about when the next person comes along—believe me.

BP: We know a place in far West Texas where the mountains are guardians to the past. A simple grocery store and a museum to a ranching family are backdrops to Celia Hill's life story, a life

APPENDIX

story she says that once completed will allow her to move on to something bigger.

CH: I'm very happy here. If somebody offered me the right amount of money, I would sell out and you know where I'd go? (Where?) I'd go where there's good fishing.
BP: As we drive away from Ruidosa it's clear the desert would never be the same without Celia.

BP: And yes, she does say it's a drive.

ACKNOWLEDGMENTS

Our special thanks go to David W. Keller, senior project archeologist at the Center for Big Bend Studies, for supplying photographs and for reading this manuscript. David made helpful improvements. We also thank Sarah Patterson, an earlier office assistant in WrightWorld, for thoughtfully reading and offering her valuable suggestions. Susan Sims (Robert's wife) added key information. We warmly thank Katherine Trotter for running down last-minute details for us. Finally, we gratefully acknowledge the contributions of Celia Hill's children Robbie Burns and her brother, James Russell "Rusty" Hill.

ABOUT THE AUTHORS

CELIA ANN HILL, 1928-2008, appears in these pages through her journals and through the memories of her friends and family.

Marianne Wood and Bill Wright. *Photo by Katherine Trotter.*

BILL WRIGHT'S photographs are in many private collections as well as in such museums as the Amon Carter in Fort Worth and the Museum of Fine Arts in Houston. He is the author of, or contributor to, twelve books.

MARIANNE WOOD holds a bachelor of fine arts degree from Texas Tech University and has taught art in museums and schools for many years. She has published articles in a number of magazines and journals.

www.ingramcontent.com/pod-product-compliance
Lightning Source LLC
Chambersburg PA
CBHW051132160426
43195CB00014B/2437